Song of the Fool

Song of the Fool

On the Road with Stephen Kellogg
and the Sixers

Hunter Sharpless

Foreword by
Stephen Kellogg

RESOURCE *Publications* · Eugene, Oregon

SONG OF THE FOOL
On the Road with Stephen Kellogg and the Sixers

Resource Publications
An Imprint of Wipf and Stock Publishers
199 W. 8th Ave., Suite 3
Eugene, OR 97401

www.wipfandstock.com

ISBN 13: 978-1-4982-0072-1

Manufactured in the U.S.A.   09/08/2014

Permissions obtained for use of any lyrics by Stephen Kellogg or Stephen Kellogg and the Sixers.

To my parents, who let their firstborn son go on the road.

In fact, my artificial style may have made the message more effective.

—*NOTES FROM UNDERGROUND*, FYODOR DOSTOEVSKY

Contents

Foreword

I'VE HEARD IT SAID that "youth is wasted on the young," but I've never found that to be the case. Youth is the necessary condition that keeps us going as we stumble our way through the gates of early adulthood, failing miserably and often. Still, in flashes and on good days we can also feel the rush and energy of what we later arrogantly call "accomplishment." If I had known then what I know now, then what happened then wouldn't have been what it was, and that would have been a damn shame because what was, was awesome. I'm getting ahead of myself though, so let me take it back a moment.

My grandfather had a great axiom he used to share with me: "Never believe your own propaganda." Hearing him comment to that effect hundreds of times filled my brain with a healthy skepticism about what others would say of me, on both the positive and negative sides. The press, when they thought of me at all, would often write cutting reviews with the underlying message that "this guy is nothing special." Sorry mom, but they've found me out! As such I tended to think of the press, when I thought of them at all, in much the same way they thought of me. Nothing special.

On the flip side it was also easy to assume that anyone with a positive assessment of my work was probably just friendly and it had nothing to do with my work actually being any good. A little self-destructive and kind of a messed up way to think, right? Nonetheless, these are the murky, narcissistic waters Hunter Sharpless was entering into when he approached us about touring with our virtually unknown band in 2009. Some would call it baggage but I like to think of it as awareness. After all we'd been making a living at it for a decade and who needed any more validation than that?

I guess I did.

The fact is, I was not at all sure I wanted a young guy around, judging my friends and me. I held fast to Andy Rooney's assessment that everyone thinks they could write a book "if only they had the time." Having attempted to write one myself on multiple occasions, I realized it was harder than it looked. All the same, the lead singer in me felt a level of validation even from the whisper that someone had chosen our work to write about. I wanted to believe in Hunter. I just didn't want to be hurt by being misunderstood or ignored (by the very real possibility that the book would never actually get written), and I didn't want to be the subject of a "puff piece"—something I know all too well wouldn't be representative of the man I am.

I needn't have worried. In the book we all come off, including the author himself, as a little damaged but ultimately decent. Most of *Song of the Fool* is composed of material I had no idea was being observed. The moments that fit more in the cracks. They weren't the high highs or even the low lows of the road—this was the everyday stuff. And the everyday stuff is sometimes all we have in life, so we've got an obligation to make the most of it. I remembered that while reading this book.

So yeah, Hunter's a young guy, but that's what makes his memoir special. No one told him that you don't write books about underground cult bands that perhaps will only be read by diehard fans. You don't write memoirs of what it's like to be a suburban-raised, well loved teenager traveling with a painfully normal bunch of guys who treat their band as their business, guided by an affable girl with a great sense of humor. All the edges that the media and buying public crave are missing. No one told him this or if they did he didn't listen (also a trademark of youth).

Thank goodness they didn't, because what resulted is a snapshot of real stuff. Authentic stuff. The stuff that makes up all of our days. No, youth isn't wasted on the young. It's lathered on the young in the hopes that someone will do things that haven't been done yet and use their superpowers for good. That someone will illuminate the truth. I hope that others can learn from some of our mistakes and enjoy the reading of this story half as much as I enjoyed the living of it.

Stephen Kellogg
June 2014

This started as I sat in a freshman seminar on the American short story at the University of Iowa. I was bored and had very lofty ideas and so I thought to myself, The days of unreal dreams are over, and then I emailed them and asked if I could write a book about them. But there is the story of Moses who struck the rock out of which water flowed abundantly, and like Moses I felt, when they responded, I had struck something wonderful and was swimming freely. The things I had dreamed about were now incarnate and, also like Moses, I thought naïvely there was the water and nothing else.

1

Skunk

IN THE MIRROR I saw myself: young, skinny, and pale as paper, with black hairs like stray words scattered across my chest.

I didn't think Stephen would choose me.

I didn't feel able. I was nineteen years old and had never in my life set up a stage, had never driven across the country, had never known the sleepless and endless wanderings of the show.

It was five in the morning and I was dressing to fly from Dallas, my home, to Atlanta, where I would rent a car and drive to Charlottesville, Virginia, nine hours away. Finding a car had been difficult, my mother and I sitting at the computer, searching first Charlottesville, then the state of Virginia, and finally the entire southeastern region of the United States. We found EZ-Car Rental in Atlanta.

After signing waivers and receiving the keys, I sped out of the airport in a brown sedan. My mind was occupied with thoughts of proving to Stephen that I could be a worthy roadie. That maybe I could be a guitar tech or do merchandise, anything productive. I wondered what sort of person a roadie ought to be. I had read books and had seen movies about touring, but did not know if I fit the description. I was not especially grungy and I did not do drugs. When I was just past the city I realized I could not find the GPS device my mother had ordered for the car. It was not in the glove compartment. I picked up my phone.

"Is this EZ-Car Rental?" I asked.

"Yes," a voice said, the voice of the man from whom I had received the car keys, a bald and muscular man who had sized me up with a frown and who had—when I'd called attention to a scratch on the car, per my mother's instructions—written SCRATCHES AND SCUFFS ALL OVER on the report.

"What do you want?" he asked.

"Um, yes," I said. "Good, well, I ordered a GPS device for the car?" I allowed my voice to trail off.

"And?" he said.

"And it's not in the car."

"Sir, turn around."

I looped back and restarted my journey. I looked again to Atlanta's cityscape. Skyscrapers reminding me of Dallas turned to suburbs turned to yellow-green fields and farms, then small hills and, past them, forests with tall trees. I was on Interstate 85 north, through South Carolina and into North Carolina, through North Carolina and into Virginia, lastly creeping into the Blue Ridge Mountains.

The Omni Hotel was situated by a pedestrian mall, a red-brick arcade busy with summer people, the lengths of the arcade lined with bars, old theaters and boutique shops. I crossed the red bricks of the mall and walked through the glass doors of the hotel and into the elevator, then pressed for the seventh floor. These were the instructions I had been given by Jessica, the band's tour manager and Stephen's cousin; I had met her once before. She was blunt and seemed to be very in charge of things. The doors shut and I saw my reflection: sandals, cut-off khaki shorts, a white shirt and a straw fedora. I had meticulously chosen this unintentional-looking wardrobe and was very proud of myself. The whole ensemble, I thought, evoked Tom Sawyer. I was adventurous, and a little edgy. None of this, of course, was true. I had gone to a private classical school where we had translated modest excerpts of *The Aeneid* in junior high, I had never scored below a B in a class, and I was well known for my unrivaled speed in multiplication and division worksheets. But Sawyer was an impressive persona. The hat, however, a less-than-ten dollar purchase from a thrift store, was the real crowning achievement.

Never in my life before that day had I worn a fedora, but after watching a series of videos the band had posted on their website in which each member was wearing one, and in an attempt to create a sense of serendipitous solidarity, I wore it as casually as I could. The band—Stephen Kellogg and the Sixers—was composed of four members, each of whom had a nickname. Stephen, the lead singer and frontman, was sometimes known as Skunk. The Sixers were Brian, Sam, and Kit, alternately named Boots, Steamer, and Goose. Boots, the drummer, was exclusively called by his nickname. Sam played the electric guitar and the pedal steel. And Kit played the bass guitar and keyboard. The band was not young. Stephen was in his thirties and they were, that fall, releasing their fourth studio album. I had never heard their music—had never even heard of the band—until six months earlier, when a friend told me I might like their catchy mix of Americana, pop and folk-country. He said I would certainly like their shows. I bought an album and listened. The Sixers, it seemed, wrote songs about fatherhood and junior high memories and family. The music I was listening to at the time was not about these things.

I knocked.

"Hunter!" Jessica said excitedly, opening the door. Her hair was brown and curly all over her head. "We're glad you made it—hope the drive was okay."

She hugged me and I shuffled into the room, set my bags down, and stood. Stephen sat on one of the two beds in the room, the backscreen of his laptop illuminating his face.

"Hey pal," he said, looking over. He was very skinny. He had shaggy brown hair like his cousin. Then he said, "Almost forgot you were coming."

This worried me immensely. I had driven nine hours, five hundred miles across a sizable portion of the south, this after renting a car from a man with very big arms and a very short temper, this after flying from Dallas to Atlanta, and all of this, finally, after waking up before five that morning. I said nothing, knowing that the interview process was just now starting. When Stephen got up from the bed and came over to me, I stuck out my hand and mentally prepared to give a firm but not throttling squeeze, but in my handshake preoccupation I did not notice that he had spread his arms wide in order to hug me; thus I jabbed him sharply in the stomach before we floundered into an embrace. "You hungry?" he quickly asked.

Jessica led Stephen and me out of the hotel and into the pedestrian mall. It was dusk. The neon signs advertising the many restaurants were beginning to flicker on.

"I was thinking sushi," Stephen said casually.

Jessica looked alert and said, "I think I remember a place over here." She walked ahead of us.

I tried valiantly to be the first to locate Japanese characters that might indicate sushi, swiveling my head to one side of the mall and then the other, not noticing that Jessica had already found the place.

"Fuck," Stephen said, approaching the doors and shaking them. "It's closed."

"That's bullshit," I offered in support. I acted as exasperated as he looked. (I had, in actuality, never tried sushi.)

We instead ate burgers and French fries. A plaque on the wall announced that the place had received the BEST VALUE award for Charlottesville the year before. I ate my food quietly while watching Stephen who, in a matter of minutes, ordered, unwrapped, and finished both a grilled cheese sandwich and a double cheeseburger. In my life I had not seen many people skinnier than Stephen and had had the impression—after his desire for sushi—that perhaps he was a man of salads and other refined meals. After dinner we watched a documentary on Neil Young and returned to the hotel, where I was to be sharing a room with them. I was nervous and while I urinated I could hear their nearby voices. I crawled into bed to the sound of tapping keyboards.

The next morning Jessica woke me by pushing aside the curtain and spilling sunlight into the room. I could hear Stephen running the sink, brushing his teeth.

"Hey Jess," he said through the cracked door. "Do I want to shower right now?"

She cocked her head.

"Well," she said. "No. Because you'll probably want to work out and then shower before the show tonight."

Stephen was to play at a local radio station that morning. I did not know if they wanted me there or not.

"So," I said. Sitting up in bed I looked at Jessica. She looked at me and waited. "Am I staying here?"

"No. You're driving us."

Stephen sat in the backseat, Jessica fit his acoustic guitar in the trunk at an angle, and I gripped the steering wheel tightly, my hands conforming to the leather. When both were in the car Stephen said, "Now we get to see what your parents are so freaked out about."

Sometime the night before I had mentioned that only days before the trip I had wrecked my family's SUV by backing into a pole in a parking lot.

As they laughed together and buckled their seatbelts I checked my mirrors. Turned the wheel. And pulled out of the parking lot. I drove with quick, fumbling hands, with a light-and-heavy foot, maneuvering the car either much too fast or much too slow, and when we finally reached the parking lot safely, the only space available was one in which I had to parallel park. I failed a first and second time. Then Stephen exited the car. I did not know what he was doing, if he was frustrated or simply done with me. He said to roll down the window. I did. He said he would help me park. He stood a few feet away from the car and said, "A little more, a little more . . . nope . . . okay, almost, yes!" motioning his hands, helping me gradually bring the car to a stop.

The radio station was undergoing renovations. Or it was going under altogether. There was tape on various doors. There were handwritten instructions. There was free water in the lobby. A receptionist led us to a studio, from which there appeared a small man, the DJ, who proceeded to take Stephen inside the closet-sized room with two microphones, shelves of CDs, and a cluttered desk.

Jessica and I watched through a pane of glass. She asked about my thoughts on the book. I had met the band briefly the spring before, and in the months between then and now had read, as research, books by Lester Bangs on Van Morrison, books on Abraham Lincoln, books on The Band, books on punk rock, books on the parallels and later differences in the careers of Neil Young and Bruce Springsteen, and other books. Some of these books were recommended by Stephen, and some not, but the sum total of my reading had instilled in me a sort of papier-mâché belief that I knew what I was doing. Now, I thought, I am an aspiring author. I really know something about music. I was not afraid to insert casually into conversation facts and very staunch opinions about the MC5 or the tragic heroism of Richard Manuel or Abraham Lincoln's depression. I was very sure of things. Jessica looked vaguely interested.

When we had returned to the hotel Stephen and I sat down to lunch.

He was from Connecticut, I was from Texas.

He could play the guitar, and he could write songs, and he could sing them, and he could play the kazoo, and he could crack jokes and make women swoon with stories. I had certainly never made a woman swoon.

He was married, I was a teenager.

He had completed college ten years ago. I was done with year one. His favorite book was *David Copperfield*. I hated Charles Dickens. My favorite book was *A Farewell to Arms*. He said his grandfather, who had been in a platoon during the Second World War covered by Hemingway, could not stand the Nobel-winning alcoholic.

Stephen was a great orator. During shows he commanded the ability to seduce crowds into laughter or silence, an ability evident with or without his band. In a bar in Austin, Texas, he, alone on stage with his guitar, lulled a boisterous crowd of 300 into silence, bartenders and all; the song was about sleeping soundly, about his wife, about his daughters.

He had two daughters; more were coming soon. I did not have children.

He liked Maker's Mark whiskey; I had not yet tried it.

I didn't know how to string or play or tune a guitar, and I didn't know how to drive a van and trailer, and I didn't know how to live in hotel after hotel and I did not know how to make a crowd sing my own words by heart; all these things, he knew.

In high school the name of his band was Silent Treatment. He attended an all boy's school and one year at a dance, a dance at which there were girls from the sister school, he saw Kirsten across the floor. They were both there because of their involvement with student council. He thought she was beautiful. He wooed her by driving his orange Hyundai Excel from his suburban home to Greenwich, Connecticut. While he drove he listened to Whitesnake and Scorpions and Mötley Crüe. In college he grew his hair out, listened to the Grateful Dead, and played at keg parties. Then he lived in a cabin in the woods, selling advertisements for a magazine. And then he married the girl.

I was single.

He had a name: Stephen Kellogg. His name was on the Internet and in magazines and newspapers and occasionally on TV programs and it was on the front of records.

I had no name.

He had a nickname: Skunk. It was not a flattering name but it was a name.

I was no one. But I told him I had an idea for a book about his band. And he listened.

"I want you on the road," he said.

Two hours later, I wore a fat smile as I paid the parking attendant in front of Is Venue. Stephen was opening for Dar Williams, a middle-aged folk musician active since the early 90s.

"Who's playing tonight?" the attendant asked.

"Dar Williams and Stephen Kellogg," I said, smiling still.

He grunted as he took the dollar bills.

"They're really great. Thank you, sir."

I crossed the street and saw Dar's tour bus. It was big, gray-blue and shiny, with dark-green streaks. It was grand-looking. Stephen was probably in there right now. He was probably in there warming up his voice or having a drink. I saw Jessica unloading some tubs of CDs from underneath the bus.

"Oh hey," I said. "I guess this is my first show as a member, huh?"

She looked at me, her arms full.

"Yep. You excited?"

"So excited."

Through the front door of the venue was a dark staircase to the second floor. At the top there was a bar, stocked well with beers, liquors and snacks in baskets. To the right were two merchandise tables, one for Dar, one for Stephen. Behind was the stage, lit with red and blue lights. Guitars, amps, an accordion, a keyboard, a stool, harmonicas and microphones, but no people yet. Dim lights hanging from a low ceiling shone down on the hardwood floors, scuffed and scratched.

I paced in front of the stage, holding a camera or holding a pen and pad or holding nothing at all. Months ago I had been in school and now this. What was this? It was something I had dreamed about. That was sure. But here I was. Here was a real venue and a real show coming and there were merchandise tables which were real and free fish tacos for dinner which were real and I needed to talk to someone outside of this to make sure everything was real and there was a tour bus outside but I knew that the Sixers would not be on a bus when I joined them on tour but still there was the bus outside and I took a picture of it. And there was Dar Williams on the stage now warming up and she knew Joan Baez and Joan Baez knew Bob Dylan and Bob Dylan was Bob Dylan. Dar was a real folk musician. And there she was, middle-aged and still pretty and nice and now getting off the stage. And there was Carolyn, her tour manager, with her short-cropped hair and a rough way of talking. I'd heard Carolyn had been Patty Griffin's tour manager.

Then I heard through the microphone: "Hey, bud."

And there was Stephen.

His guitar was now plugged into the amp and I could see his toes sticking out of his flip-flops at the bottom of his jeans.

I snapped the lens of the camera and looked up at him.

Soon the show began, the room now full of people. The crowd was mostly middle-aged, and their clothes were colors like a host of flags or garden of flowers. Colorful and patterned clothes, long dresses. I saw women with hair down to their torsos. Hoop earrings. When Stephen took the stage, they clapped, then hushed. He had a brown guitar and a silver harmonica holder around his neck. The music started and the crowd was admirably attentive, reverent during the ballads, laughing at his jokes, applauding rigorously after each song.

It was quiet, and I was quiet, and then, while Stephen's eyes were turned down to the tuning pedal, a fragile voice in the crowd said something indistinguishable.

Stephen looked up and said, "What was that?"

The voice spoke up again. It was a girl. Her voice was stronger now. She was requesting a certain song.

Stephen said, "Okay," and as he stepped away from the microphone his hand dipped across the strings of the guitar, the notes sounding softly at first, and bright, then sewn together, the song a single sound, and as I watched I saw a tightening of the facial muscles that looked like a grimace or a flash of pain. The words began.

> I guess I gave it up then
> This self that eludes weaker men
> What was my young heart to do?
> A girlfriend as pretty as you

As he sang I could see that this crowd not only watched him play, watched his hand across the guitar, watched the contortions of his face, but they listened.

One month later I sat in the back bench of the van, listening to Stephen incite his band for the tour, which started the next day. They had just rehearsed at a venue called StageOne in Fairfield, Connecticut.

"We need to play from a place that's fucking joyful," he was saying, "from the inside out."

It was dark. Boots, Kit and Sam listened and watched. They were silent. As Stephen spoke he locked eyes with each, one by one. His eyes were hungry like fire, theirs like kindling.

"It's okay to make mistakes," he said. "But we've got to know our shit. It's our responsibility to play the music no matter what. Keep getting up. Every night. Every morning."

He looked at Sam.

"They want more Steamer. Don't be afraid."

It was Sam's first tour as an official member of the band. He had played shows with them before but he did not have a name with the fans. They did not know him, Stephen said, but they wanted to. Sam's job in those months was to earn himself a name, to find his place.

The van in which we sat was named the Bear, named both for its golden color, which grew dirty and dark with dust from the road, and for the album the Sixers had just released. *The Bear* was their fourth studio album. Following the release of their debut in 2004, *Bulletproof Heart*, they were signed by Universal Records who, in 2005, released the band's self-titled *Stephen Kellogg and the Sixers*. Two years later they released *Glassjaw Boxer* with a subsidiary label and were currently signed with Vanguard Records. I did not know the exact numbers of records sold but I knew they rode in a van and not a bus and that they played, in some places, dive bars rather than theaters and I wondered why their music had not sold more.

There were four benches in the Bear. Stephen, Boots, Sam and Kit each had one as his own. Jessica and I did not; we were displaced. We occupied the benches of whoever was driving and riding passenger. Sam's bench was the first, Stephen's was the second, and Boots' was the third. He was called Boots like a cat because he slept heavily and often. He was quiet and had dark, beady eyes and I was afraid of him. Kit had the last bench. When I met him his hair had been blonde. Now it was black.

The van was public. I learned this. They pissed in bottles, they drank coffee, made phone calls, wrote, watched movies on their laptops, slept, or they read. I myself could neither piss nor read without getting embarrassed or sick, so I mostly listened to music or slept, always half-awake. Sometimes I read anyways, until my stomach turned.

Not once in three months did I piss in a bottle.

I remember receiving my first serious task. I was to secretively procure a birthday cake.

We were in Northampton, Massachusetts. It was the third show of the tour.

I was sitting quietly on the couch in Jessica's living room when I felt my pocket vibrate. It was a text message from Stephen, who sat a few feet away in the same room. He looked at me with his brown eyes and winked. I was delighted. How sly! I read the message, then inconspicuously declared to the room that I needed to make a phone call. I stepped outside and contacted La Fiorentina, a bakery near the venue. Before the show started I went to pick up the cake. There were patrons sitting at small circular tables and pretty, dark-haired girls working the counter.

I said, "Hi, uh."

One of the girls looked at me.

And I said, "Hi, I, uh, ordered a coffee cake." She was very pretty.

"A cappuccino cake," she corrected. "Do you want anything written on it?"

"'Happy Birthday Boots and Jessica,'" I said.

"Is Boots a cat?"

"No."

"Oh."

At the right moment during the set—Stephen had instructed me on two separate occasions—I was to bring the cake, candles lit, from the back of the venue up to the stage, thus rallying the audience into the spontaneous singing of "Happy Birthday" to Boots and Jessica. Their birthday was on the same day.

When it was time, a waitress wearing a Mets shirt helped me light the candles with a lighter she had pulled from the pocket of her blue jeans. The cake, on a circular tray, was heavy. Other

13

members of the wait staff watched us light the candles. We were all in on the surprise. The Sixers were ending a song on stage. This was it. I started walking and the candles went out. She lit the candles again and said "Hurry!" and I was handed a tray to help shield the fire from the flow of air. I started again. It was dark. People drank beer. The show was sold-out. As I walked through the crowd people said things like, "Oh, look!" or "A cake?" or "A cake!" and I felt the same gradual rise of excitement in the audience that I had felt with the wait staff and I walked proudly knowing that I, like a great bard, had inspired the people.

I saw Stephen looking at me. I beamed, happy with myself. Then the sound stopped and I saw him make a face. He said very clearly into the microphone, "Nope. Put the cake away, kid. Next song." He cracked a joke to save the mistake and the crowd laughed at me but I could not hear as I was retreating. I had delivered the cake at the wrong time.

The horror!

"Sharpless," Stephen said to me in a dressing room in Annapolis, Maryland. "Can you do me a favor?"

"All right, Skunk," I said. "What is it?"

He explained that he needed me to buy a gift for his wife. It was Kirsten's birthday this weekend and though he had purchased something large already, he wanted something small too. He handed me a twenty-dollar bill.

The sky was cloudless and blue, the sun a light-bulb yellow. I aimed to do my task well, for Stephen, for Kirsten. Walking across the red-brick road I remembered the times I had met Kirsten. The first was after she had dropped off Sophia, their eldest daughter, from school. Kirsten wore a t-shirt and windbreaker pants, but she was pretty. She had long dark hair and milky skin. And she was very kind. And then I had met her again at the first show of the tour in Connecticut, near the Kellogg's home, and this time she wore pressed jeans, a black top, and a turquoise scarf.

I had seen an antique store earlier, toward which I was now walking, a place I thought ideal for buying a gift. But on my way I saw a bookstore. I altered directions, crossed the street. I had time for myself before I went to the antique store. Opening the door I could smell the papery, dusty smell of books. There were old books, their jackets slightly splayed, their ink fading, and there were new books, unworn, bright, crisp and eager. I wandered for a while, then brooded reverently by Hemingway. A particularly beautiful copy of *A Farewell to Arms* stuck out. It was from 1957. It was blue-jacketed with a fringed spine, some threads loose. I opened it: "When I saw her I was in love with her. Everything turned over inside me." Then I closed it. Well, that was true. I fell in love with Catherine every time I read that book.

"I'll take this," I said at the register.

The woman asked if I was a student at St. John's, one of the two universities in Annapolis. The other was the Naval Academy. I wore a beard, tight jeans, and a v-neck shirt that exposed my chest hairs. I did not look like a military man. I told her I was a student at the University of Iowa.

"Iowa?"

Iowa.

"Well," she said. "Why are you here?"

I explained.

"What sort of band?" she asked.

The answer I had grown accustomed to giving was the answer I gave. "Roots rock," I said, and then mentioned influences like Jackson Browne, Cat Stevens, Tom Petty. When I was asked this question I juggled a number of phrases: "roots-rock-pop," and sometimes "they're like a mixture of roots-rock, Americana, pop, and Stephen's voice has a sort of twang to it," and then I'd give the names, which gave us historical and cultural proportions, explaining that the question of genre was diminutive and reductive. I was proud to be with a band that evaded neat distinctions, but I was also embarrassed that there was no real answer. What could I say?

I could tell them he wrote songs about his daughters and his wife, and that they were a "mid-success" kind of band. People gauged success in a number of ways, the lowest degree of which was whether the band was signed to a record label. They were. Then there was the question of what kind of label. Not the biggest, and seemingly always switching. And finally there was the actual name of the band. Stephen Kellogg and the Sixers. There were three responses to this. The first—and most rare—was that the person had heard of the band. Suddenly they brightened with happiness—and sometimes jealousy—and listed a number of songs and lyrics and facts. If they had heard of the Sixers, they often knew more of the band's history than I did. The second response was that they had not heard of them but were interested; this was the most common. And the last was the same fact—"I haven't heard of them"—inflected with a different tone, a tone that said, "I haven't heard of them, so they probably are neither very good nor very important."

"Let me see here," the woman said. We were quiet as she clicked away at the computer. Then I heard the opening piano to "Sweet Sophia," the first track of the Sixers' third record, *Glassjaw Boxer*. Her eyes narrowed as she stared hard at the computer screen. Then she commenced to bob her head up and down with the rhythm.

"I like it!" she declared, but when she asked about the show, when she was just becoming enthused, I told her it was sold-out. I thanked her and went across the street.

I lost some credibility with the saleswoman at the antique shop when I confessed my twenty-dollar budget. "Well feel free to look around," she said cordially and coldly, and then walked away. Having bought, in my life, an exorbitant amount of candles, charms and candlesticks for my mom, I decided on a jar. It, I thought, was beautiful: milky and blue and translucent. And it was only twelve dollars. And I had rescued it from a forgotten place on a bottom shelf, among many other jars not quite as beautiful as this one. I returned to the venue with the jar and with scissors, tape, and thread I took the small note that Stephen had written for

Kirsten and created a message-in-a-bottle. Like a child I presented my work to Stephen.

A fog concealed the hills. Like a skier carving moguls our van carved the land. The hills and valleys and mountains and bluffs were thickly covered with green forests and brush. There was no distinction between the gray of the fog and the gray of the clouds. There were streams here or there, with beds of gray stones, the water clean, steady and quick. Off the interstate we drove by white steeples and red-brick houses, immaculately kept. In a town like this we found the college at which we were to play.

Before the set I sat against the corner of the stage. Then I saw someone, presumably a student of Middlebury College, walking this way with a lanky stride, his arms swinging by his sides, his flip-flops clapping the sidewalk. He wore a Detroit Red Wings jersey. He saw me and asked how I was doing. I said I was fine. Then he said, "You're living the dream."

I knew the dream he was referring to because it had been my dream to tour with a band that played good music and now I was touring with a band that played good music but the dream was turning out to be different than I had imagined. When the Sixers started the show fewer than twenty people made up the audience. I sat in a small lonely town in Vermont on a picnic table in the lawn of a small college. I saw a brown lawn chair next to a red lawn chair next to a green lawn chair. They were all empty. On the table there was a gray coffee mug. There was a bike rack nearby with nine bikes, three of which had baskets. A handwritten sign announced the show was, that afternoon, FREE.

But the music started. The music started and I forgot my worries. During the set it rained lightly and Stephen looked at me as I stood to the side of the stage covering his electric guitar with my shirt. He shrugged his shoulders, keeping his eyes on mine while still singing the song. And at least for a moment I felt free.

One night I slept on the floor of Stephen's living room. I was given an old and worn blanket covered in Smurfs. "It was Stephen's when he was a kid," I was told, and then I slept.

In the morning I woke to screaming, at first high-pitched and sharp, then subsiding into a defeated whimper. I knew it was one of Stephen's daughters. The scream came from the kitchen, a few rooms away, and I rose from the air mattress, found a towel in the bathroom and showered. I oriented myself the way one does in another's shower, acquainting myself with another man's shampoo, with his strange soap, with the quality of showerhead he was able to afford.

In the kitchen Adeline, the younger of Stephen's two daughters, sat in a high-chair. She flared her blue eyes at me. The skin surrounding her eyes was red and puffy from the crying, making the irises a pulsating blue. She momentarily paused her screaming to appraise me, but soon returned to it.

"Good morning, Hunter," Stephen said, smiling profusely, standing in the middle of the kitchen. He wore nothing but boxer shorts. He was a wiry frame covered in hair—unkempt on the top of his head, scattered across his back and shoulders, thick on his chest. He continued his parley with Adeline, who seemed hungry and thirsty but unwilling to eat or drink what was in front of her. Stephen spoke to her in a very frank and kind manner and she, being two years old, answered in honest and passionate tears.

Stephen offered me tea. "If you come to the Kellogg house," he said, "we'll offer you tea. Go pick one out and I'll get you a mug with hot water."

Adeline continued to wail.

When we left New England for the road they—Stephen's daughters, even while remaining in Connecticut—stayed with us, like muses, like ghosts. They were in his songs—"Sweet Sophia," "Oh Adeline," and "Father's Day"—and they were on the phone. They were on the computer screen and they were on his mind. He spoke with his daughters every day during the tour. Sometimes they would be sobbing, unhappy about going to sleep, sad their dad was gone, and sometimes they were delighted, filled with joy. In the van, at a coffee shop, in a hotel room or lobby, at restaurants, in airports, on trains—he spoke with them everywhere and always. And each time, I think, it hurt him, but they were always with him and by extension, with us, with the band. Even at radio stations with tattooed DJs wearing political shirts, they were with us.

Brother Wease, as he was known on air, wore glasses, headphones that covered his ears entirely, and several rings. His voice was loud. Surrounded by other microphones with other people wearing other headphones, Brother Wease sat in the center of the studio.

"So who's this fraternity kid?" he asked during commercial break, pointing to me.

I wore a sorority t-shirt. I looked to Stephen for help.

Stephen, also wearing headphones, laughed, because this was not the first time I had been noticed and subsequently questioned at a radio station. Stephen explained I was a student writing a book. A "young writer," he said. Or sometimes an "aspiring author." This was a farce but I went on with it, always holding my pen and notepad as if to provide evidence.

Brother Wease asked me to tell an interesting story on air after the commercial break. A microphone was thrust in front of my face. I joined the round table of men and women with headphones.

I knew what he meant when he said "interesting," but I also knew I didn't have that. I did not have stories about blowjobs or alcohol or orgies or heroin. All I had were stories about gas stations and hotels, meals at Applebee's, stories about unloading the trailer again and again, through another door at a different angle, with or without help, stories with the same five people. They were my stories, but I did not think they'd be his. So I told what I had, which was playing dolls with Sophia at Stephen's house. "Snow White it's so nice to see you!" she had said to me. At the radio station as I told the story I tried to be funny, but no one laughed, tried to be endearing, but no one cooed. I couldn't frame these stories. Couldn't fit them into complete sentences. Whatever conventions I had been handed by movies or books or people were wrong, in fact profane. As soon as it had come from my mouth I felt guilty, guilty and silly for not participating in a sort of game of confirmed anticipations, and as soon as Brother Wease heard it he redirected the conversation to I do not remember because I was feeling guilty. But then it came around. And he, this tattooed DJ, was talking about his own children, explaining how they were so cute he wanted to eat them, explaining that sometimes he did in fact nibble their soft skin. He played "Oh Adeline" and "Sweet Sophia" and the program ended.

"It's nice to know the worth of water," sings Stephen in one of the songs about his daughters, "before the well runs dry."

Once, Sophia came to a show. She scuttled about the dressing room, in the basement of the Iron Horse in Northampton, Massachusetts. She sought our attention, our eyes, as she danced around the room pretending to be a monster or forming her hands into a jellyfish. She'd sting someone, step back, anticipating their reaction, and when they'd cry out in imaginary pain she would burst into giggles.

"God, I love that sound," Stephen said, sitting on a couch. He was writing the set list for the show. He watched his daughter.

She came up to me and asked for a story. I held my hands together, palms up, making an open book, and told a story after which she told her own. There was a dragon, a princess, and a castle.

The morning after that show we were to leave New England. We had played shows close to home but it was now time to take the road away from here. Northampton was busy with the clear and cold morning rush. People rode bikes, rode buses, drove cars, walked, smoked, bought coffee, talked on phones, opened doors, closed them, took elevators, ate breakfast, went to meetings. The Bear was parked and packed. Sophia and I stood by a flowerbed. She picked some flowers and handed them to me. When she walked, her brown curls bounced. I did not know if she knew that we, and her dad with us, were leaving. But when the doors of the van opened and when we climbed inside one by one, and when her dad hugged her, kissed her, and climbed in the van after us, she knew.

Leaving New England and riding west, the weight of our journey was in front of us, like a book when you have just started, the pages heavy in your right hand, light in your left. We rode west. The land moved fast. The hills, farms and cities never stopped. I watched it all roll by. Well, I thought, now I am on the road.

I was sick, and sat in the lobby of the Majestic Theater in Madison, Wisconsin, looking through the window to the rain.

Inside, the Sixers were rehearsing for their show. From the stage they would have been looking at a high ceiling, a fine balcony, and cream and crimson walls. The stage itself was framed by an intricate golden trim. Toward the back of the venue there was a bar, and past this was the lobby, where a small box office opened up to a room of large windows. Outside the sky was dark and gray and I, watching the rain smear across the glass, could not tell where the sun was, as the sky glowed one full muted color.

I had never considered being sick on the road. I had not expected it, had overlooked it. I could not breathe through my nose. The only time, I thought, you heard of sickness on the road, serious or otherwise, was when, occasionally, a show or tour was cancelled. You read about it on the band's website. But I never anticipated being sick myself, and sat thinking about the countless shows people must have played while reasonably sick. When I woke up that morning discovering my sickness, I was instantly irritable and embarrassed. I did not have the energy to put on a show about how excited I was to unload the trailer or set up the stage. I was ready to fold, did not want to keep going. When I am sick I am embarrassed because I become the person I am when all appearances and cordialities disappear. I am a boy who wants to be alone but who also wants people to know how alone he is. I thought about it. A boy, I thought. You are a boy, I said to myself. I knew it and hated it. Then I marched into the venue and told them I was off to the pharmacy, off in the rain. It was well into the afternoon and I had eaten nothing, doubling my body's lethargy. I ate pizza, bought a vitamin C concoction at the pharmacy, and after passing the capitol building and reentering the Majestic, I paced the lobby, again watching the rain, waiting for Holly, my cousin, who was coming to the show.

I had learned from living in Iowa that Midwestern girls—unless they were from Chicago, and sometimes even then—dreamed of either California or New York. I knew one who had gone to Florida but she seemed to be the exception. The more moderate ones chose Arizona. Holly was from Wisconsin, and she wanted to go to New York City. *The City.* That was what they called it. That was its name. *The Big Apple.* A very smart girl studying actuarial science, very pretty, and very driven, Holly dreamed of Manhattan. Though, she had told me, she had apprehensions. With Holly there was always the tension between the desire to go and the desire to stay, an in-between of Here and There. We talked of these and other things when I greeted her inside the lobby. She held a turquoise umbrella. Her cheeks were flushed with red. She smiled brightly. I had not seen her for a long time, and she was the first family I had welcomed on the road as a member of this side of the show, the side of the performer. To speak with someone I knew—with family—was strange. It had been three weeks of the Sixers and a collection of minor characters: gas station clerks, club managers, and sound techs. Holly and I talked until I needed to go backstage.

And so I left Holly, left the audience, left the high ceilings and framed view of the stage, walked down some stairs, through a door, and crouched while the Sixers played the music. What I saw had changed. I could see the Sixers playing their instruments, turned toward the audience, and if I leaned out over the stage, I could see the intent faces watching them.

During the show, I waited. I waited to catch the eyes of the Sixers in case they needed something, maybe a towel to wipe away sweat, because they sweat profusely while they played, maybe a message relayed to Jessica, or maybe a whiskey.

My fear was that people I knew—like Holly—or even people I did not know—the fans of the Sixers, with whom I sometimes interacted and who, on more than one occasion, asked for my autograph on merchandise they had purchased—my fear was that everyone—worst of all, the Sixers themselves—would see through my charade.

I did nothing of significance. I was mostly useless. There was not much movement—even physical movement—in what I did and did not do during the show. I was static. When I told others what I was doing—sailing around America with a rock band—it sounded golden. It was all very cinematic. "It's like a movie!" they'd say, over and over. I told people I was writing a book. I had introduced myself to the band as a writer. But I had never written anything. And I did not know how to write. But it was an impressive enough part to play. I am static, I thought as I crouched to the side of the stage. I am static anticipation. What do I do? I get them coffee and I retrieve their wardrobe bags from the van like a dog. All there was was the still and restless and repetitive fear that something might go wrong and I, not knowing anything about how it worked, would make things worse. The fear that Stephen would look past my eyes and directly into my staged lie. The fear that I would be held responsible for who I was not.

In the beginning I oscillated between a feeling of worship and a feeling of total disdain for the actual show. The music was the only thing that could carry the weight of being on the road—the little sleep, the long drives, the homelessness—but it was what turned me inside-out, left me raw. No one saw what I did during the show; they expected I was doing important things. By association I was important.

But, inevitably, each set moved on. Each set moved from beginning to middle to end despite my inertness. Everyone knew the script. The Sixers knew it and the audience knew it and now I could see both sides of it and I did not know what I knew.

We had been on the road for a couple weeks.

The green and yellow fields rolled up and down outside the window. Clusters of trees were scattered on hillsides. We drove through small towns, past elementary schools and post offices.

This was Iowa. I had not seen her in months. I had not seen my friends, had not seen my town. I was on the road, on the road with people about whom I knew little, nice people but still strangers. In those first weeks I felt hollow and alone but I knew it and that was easy enough to deal with but now, in Iowa, I was hollow and close to everything I loved at the same time. But they were coming. My friends, to the show, in a silver sedan.

As soon as I helped unload the trailer at the venue, I took a walk.

The sky was dark gray, the clouds hanging low. Soon it was raining. And soon after that I could smell the sweet smell of the raindrops on the pavement as I walked down Main Street. My brown sandals darkened when I stepped in puddles. My jeans grew heavy.

Inside a coffee shop there were retro couches and brightly colored cushioned chairs and yellow wallpaper. It was a comfortable place and clean and well-lighted, and there were two children by the window watching the rain, which fell down now in thick sheets.

The girl behind the counter had a plain but beautiful face. She had light brown hair and cool eyes. She was the kind of Iowa I remembered.

"Hi," she said. "Can I get you something?"

I miss you, I wanted to say. I wanted to say I'm a Texan but Iowa I really loved. She took me and I loved her for that and I'd once thought Iowa was no place for people with ambition but I learned soon enough and I have crossed many state lines, I wanted to say, with Iowa on my mind.

"Hi," I said, "three cups of coffee."

The venue was called the Hub. It was a wholly unimpressive place, quite plain besides an enormous light fixture above the stage. I paced, waiting for my friends. I paced from the green room in the basement up a staircase, a stair in the middle creaking low with my step, to the stage and lights, then to another room with booths and tables and a bar, all the while checking my phone, checking the door.

When they arrived, I threw my hands up in the air, and the world became just us.

We squeezed into a booth. We talked at first of the tour. Where had I been?

I had been many places, and that was fine and interesting, but I tried to explain this wasn't like *Almost Famous*; I tried to explain that in *Almost Famous* there were drugs and sold-out stadiums and there was the *Rolling Stone* and Lester Bangs and because it was a movie instead of showing the drives which were almost intolerable hours of gray interstate they simply cut to the next scene and were there on the stage again. And there was Penny Lane. There was certainly no Penny Lane for me, no groupie to discover and fall in love with and receive meaning from. And I could not cut to the next scene when we had to drive seven hours simply to play at a used record store. I watched every exit sign. In *Almost Famous* the road was neat. Even the conflict was neat and occurred in a linear way. But really everything was a loop. Really everything was like the same record on repeat. But I wanted to talk about Iowa, about Iowa City. Iowa City was now new. It was new and strange and foreign. But before we could talk much, Jessica called.

Our set started. It started with a faulty, clunky, a cappella version of The Band's "Up On Cripple Creek," sung with Carbon Leaf, the band with whom we were touring. While Stephen led the composite group in singing, standing near the front of the stage, behind them the drummers, Boots for us and Jason for them, adjusted the kit for Boots.

The crowd was impatient.

Standing to the side of the stage, I looked for my friends. I saw them, watching as Stephen, when the a cappella had finished, strummed his electric guitar over the crowd; he was ready to be over with it. Carbon Leaf had looked halfhearted while singing. Now the crowd gave a small shout of approval, because the Sixers were playing "Start the Day Early," their drinking anthem.

> You bring the cup
> And I'll bring the moonshine

Fans of course generally liked this song, and tonight they especially liked it, the men and women with beers and cocktails, talking, talking still at the end of the song, talking through the next song until the audio spiked, faltered, crashed, Stephen's voice at first too high and then completely inaudible. Feedback screeched.

The Sixers stood in silence, holding their instruments. Stephen looked over the crowd to the booth in the back, where the sound tech tried to turn knobs and fix the situation. The crowd's chatter grew from a quiet lull to a dull roar.

Stephen squinted, yelled something, straining his voice, and cupped his hand around his ear.

He said, "Can we fix this, Jeff?"

Someone from the crowd yelled, "C'mon Jeff!"

Someone else yelled, "Woo!"

"Check, check, check," Stephen was saying into the dead microphone. "Check one two."

And someone from the crowd yelled, "Check one two!"

Shuffling my feet, I looked to Jessica, who stood, motionless, in the back by Jeff. I grabbed the cold metal handrail in front of me. I did not know what I had expected from these Iowans. Not this. They were noisy and crude. They were a mob. I watched my friends watch the scene unfold.

Then Stephen did something.

With a step toward, nod to, and inaudible word for Kit, Sam and Boots, he moved them to the front of the stage. They took out their earpieces. Off his drum kit, Boots was strapping a banjo around his back. Kit left his keyboard and retrieved an acoustic bass. And Sam and Stephen unplugged their guitars.

The crowd quieted.

The Sixers all wore t-shirts. Behind them the amps were quiet. The lights dimmed, the Sixers like a moving chiaroscuro.

When Stephen addressed the crowd, he said We.

We must be as quiet as possible.

We have a task.

We are here.

Before the sound had gone the mob was neither listening nor watching. Now its eyes were turned to him. Its ears were opened.

One corner of Stephen's mouth rose, exposing an excited flash of teeth. He pulled his baseball cap backward, rubbed his thick beard, and strummed his guitar into a smooth melody. Next to him Boots plucked his banjo, the sound high and bright and sharp over the guitar.

"Milwaukee" was beginning.

Kit swayed left and right with the bass, a light pointed directly at him, and Sam, almost in total darkness, picked his guitar.

The instruments sung together, creating a sound that slowly hushed the crowd into a quiet calm.

> And I've been chasing dreams
> In magazines the last ten years
> The way you treat your mother
> Is up to you

The song slowed, softened, until only Stephen and his guitar continued playing. This was where, on the album, the song ended. This was where we moved on to the next track.

But he kept it going. With no electricity, no piano, no drums, no electric guitar, he kept it going. And the crowd waited, listened, participated, clapping the quarter notes quietly as only Stephen moved, as he, half singing, half talking, improvised.

> Whatever seems like is going on
> Started when my mom bought the neighbor's guitar
> Started when Goose's mom
> Sent him off to learn the tuba

People laughed; Kit nodded. He'd played tuba at the University of Massachusetts, and on the title track of *The Bear* he played it too. He had even brought it out on tour: a bulky dented thing that roused the crowd when it was called upon.

> Started when Sam was homeschooled
> And just wanted to meet girls
> Started when Boots' dad said
> "Hey why don't we do something together and since
> you're a terrible athlete—"

But the audience's laughter overtook his voice, and the song finished as the Sixers joined Stephen and as the crowd joined, clapping wildly now with the quarter notes until their sound equaled or surpassed the band and when, in applause, the song had finished, the amps and vocals had been restored.

As Stephen gripped his guitar and again approached the microphone, I snapped the lens of my camera, capturing the still on the LCD screen: Stephen grinning below his brown and shaggy hair, the harmonica slung around his neck, his right hand over the strings of the guitar and his left high up on the neck, his wedding ring shining bright and reflecting the lights, his tattoo visible high up on his left arm below the sleeve of his shirt, his eyes looking into the lens.

He moved his hand. Then again, moved his hand looking at me, wanting me to come up onto the stage. My eyebrows rose. I shook my head. I mouthed, No. He smiled wider, and motioned again, and I found myself standing on stage beside him, the lights hot on my forehead, the audience a collection of dark faces.

"And he sent me this email," he was saying. He was telling them my story.

I tugged at my baby-blue shirt. Buried my hands in my jean pockets. It was very bright. I wanted to be not on the stage.

"It was his first year at school last year and he sent me this email that said, 'This feels like a lotta bullshit. Is there any way I could come out on the road with you guys? I want to write a book.'

"So we said, 'Yeah, if you want to fly out and tell us why it would be a good idea to bring an underage person out on the road who wants to write a book and is unhappy.'"

He laughed, strummed his guitar, looked at me.

"So he comes out. He's nice. He's pretty nervous about it, and he gives us this pitch and I said, 'There are so many other bands that'd be easier to be around, more fun.'

"You know, we've been out on the road together for six years. We're all best friends. It's not any easy thing to jump into. So I told him, 'Hunter, why do you want to do this?'"

He paused.

"I mean, we're not the *biggest* band in the world."

This was a great success with the audience.

"It's not really the most glamorous thing in the world. And then he sent me this email back and he said, 'It *has* to be you guys.'"

He stopped. He backed away from the microphone.

"So I said, 'Well, we're not going to pay you anything, and we're going to be assholes sometimes, and if you're going to write a book you better make sure to get that in there.' We don't need a Jonas Brothers piece here." This was another success.

"So your friend is doing a really good job, and even grew his beard out so he wouldn't get in as much trouble every time he walked into a club. But this is all real."

He looked at me.

"Are you getting what you need for a good book?"

The road wrenched from us all sanity and entertainment, so that sometimes we had to summon laughter from deep within our bowels to pass the time, laughter that was at first contrived but then as sensitive as a turned ankle, growing less reasonable the longer we sat in the van.

Our longest drive was twenty-nine hours.

We woke in a moderately luxurious hotel in St. Louis and slept late, until about nine in the morning. The GPS device predicted the drive would take only twenty-two hours, and since we did not need to be in Scottsdale, Arizona, until the next afternoon, we lounged in the lobby like lazy cats. I ate breakfast twice and bought a third for the trip.

Stephen and Boots drove the first shift, moving us past the Mississippi River, the muddy spine of our country, to the plains. After eight hours of driving our minds were already diluted enough to stop at Applebee's in Edmund, Oklahoma. The food was perfectly mediocre. The GPS, however, did not figure we would spend two hours there, staring at the collective shrine of photographs, news clippings and other mementos dedicated to Shannon Miller, an Olympic gymnast from Edmund. Nor did it figure our ultraconservative driving speeds.

We drove and drove, slowly.

We moved west, past plains and into desert.

We grew drunk with fatigue. We realized that we would not have the time to stop and sleep along the way, that we would need to drive through the night and make up time.

The sun caught up with us. I had been sleeping and sat up. It was hard to know what was what. I felt disoriented and funny. I saw a bird out the window, sitting on a fencepost.

"I fucking hate birds," I said to no one in particular.

Stephen sat up and gave me a puzzled look. His hair was matted from sleep. I saw Sam and Jessica looking at me, too, through the rearview mirror. These were the sort of comically ethereal moments that begged for someone to say something a little off.

"If that bird was tied to the fence," I said, "I would chop its head off."

For a moment they looked confused, and I, too, was trying to consider what I had said, but after several seconds our confusion spilled over into tiresome and senseless hilarity.

In Los Angeles an ex-Sixer came to the show. He was young, chatty, and good-looking. He was very successful and was only two years older than me. His name was Kyle. He had starred on Broadway and he lived in LA and he had some vague association with John Mayer. He could act and sing and play the guitar.

I sat idly while he spoke with Stephen.

Kyle was suggesting, sarcastically I think, lines with which Stephen could open the show.

"Or you could just walk up to the mic," he was saying, "and say, 'All I want is some pussy!'"

This was funny to them.

"Or, or: 'I've got a really hard cock right now.'"

They were happy.

Then Stephen asked, "You been getting some nice pussy in LA?"

"Well," Kyle said. He smiled, hesitated, snickered.

They were happy. I said nothing.

After a number of shows in California and the Pacific Northwest, we turned east. East meant home. We had been on the road two months now and had played, if you included record stores, bookstores, hospitals, radio stations and other performances, more than fifty shows.

The North Dakota landscape was gray and dead in November, moments before winter, and I saw no trees, no rivers, no mountains, no lakes, no bursting vegetation. The earth braced for snow and ice. I looked out the window to see the nothing.

That night we were playing in Fargo. It was nothing more, we thought, than a convenient stop along the way. We wished for home, for Massachusetts and Connecticut and New York, which for me meant a flight to Texas. The show, we had been told by the club's promoter, had sold nineteen tickets so far. But, he encouraged us, there would be a really good walk-up. The walk-up was the number of people who did not buy tickets beforehand but instead paid at the door. Seeing that it was a Tuesday night in Fargo, we were doubtful.

Before playing for those nineteen people, however, or before playing for those nineteen people in addition to the "really good" walk-up on what was sure to inspire a positively pulsating Tuesday night in Fargo, we stopped in Bismarck, a town of 60,000 people, to play a show at an elementary school for no pay, no commission, not even a barbeque dinner.

We set up in the gymnasium. Hanging from the high ceiling, the overhead lights shone onto the old and smooth floor. A half-circle of chairs, occupied by the teachers, faced the makeshift stage, where the Sixers stood plugging in their instruments. In the space between sat the audience, kindergarten through sixth grade. They were restlessly exuberant.

I stood outside the perimeter, watching the children.

Stephen chose the safest songs the Sixers sang, songs about not wanting to grow old or about saying goodbye to all that or about life's difficulties and joys, and he also chose "Start the Day Early," the drinking song, but for these children he, of course, altered the lyrics, so instead of singing *you bring the cup and I'll bring the moonshine*, he sang *you bring the cup and I'll bring the milkshake*. This was a roaring success with the children, who toppled over each other in mirth. When Stephen conducted an informal poll asking which flavor was the best, chocolate won. For the grand finale the Sixers jumped on each other's backs—as they sometimes did in normal shows—and spun in circles, waving goodbye, but as Stephen, on the back of Boots, faced away from the audience, we—the teachers, the schoolchildren, myself—all discovered, simultaneously, that his pants had fallen down halfway, revealing a small and pale and hairy hindquarters. One little girl shrieked, and the rest of us acted as if nothing had happened.

After the show at the elementary school, driving to Fargo with food and coffee in our laps, we talked about blowjobs. How many girls have you gotten blowjobs from? How many swallowed? Etc. I did not say anything. I had had zero blowjobs and did not know if I was proud or embarrassed. As I thought I thought I was both. I was proud and I was not proud and I was embarrassed and

I was not embarrassed. After a while Stephen said, with a smirk, "Jessica, you've been suspiciously quiet up there."

The venue in Fargo was called the Aquarium. We sat in the parking lot behind the building, on the side of which was a painted sign, from decades ago: WHITE BANNER UNIFORMS: WORK CLOTHES FOR MEN AND WOMEN. We sat in the van, waiting for nothing in particular. Stephen said, "Maybe if we don't open the door it'll just go away." This was the nineteen-ticket show. This was the 1,500-miles-from-home show. This was, as Stephen then said, "The show no one wants to play." That was the truth. That was the truth and I looked at the old sign painted on the building. Finally Jessica came and said we needed to unload. The Aquarium was a plain rectangle on the third floor of the building. With armfuls of drums and guitars and amps we passed through a door propped open by an orange cone, walked up three flights of stairs, and made the trip again. The dressing room was in the basement. There were nine TVs and several leather couches, the TVs all turned off, the couches seating our suitcases. On the floor there was a small, brown pile of dog shit. There was also a cooler, empty, with a bald eagle fronting an American flag painted on the side.

In the venue Stephen screamed in anger.

"Fuck!" he yelled. "Where's the fucking dial to my three-thousand dollar guitar?"

We looked around. We had misplaced it. Earlier we had forgotten his microphone in Bismarck, his microphone which matched his difficult-to-match voice, and now the dial was missing too.

We were headed home, home which was yet far away. We had been on the road weeks and weeks, weeks and weeks of twenty-four-hour days of radio stations and record stores and book stores and hospitals and elementary schools and theaters and bars in small towns and big cities and bustling metropolises, of eating with each other and sleeping with each other and driving together, of room 1440 or 476 or which room are we in? and now we waited aimlessly for the nineteen people to arrive.

During the set Stephen played the song he plays when nothing is going right: "Glassjaw Boxer." This was the only song I wanted to hear.

All was dark besides the three lights pointing to the stage.

"This is a song," Stephen said, "about our life the last six years."

He backed away, strummed his guitar, and then over a whining pedal steel, a dripping banjo and a breathing accordion he sang.

> We've been passed by
> You know we've been passed up
> Banged around
> But these paper hearts got tough

He wrote the song after they had been dropped by Universal. They were on their third record, pushing their luck, pushing their timing. Probability said they were done, at least with respect to making a chart-topping, thunderous entrance onto the music scene. But that was not, I thought, what they must have been playing for. They played, they recorded, and they went on the road. Again and again and again.

The crowd had grown. There were just over sixty people now.

Stephen sweat, he sang. In his eyes I saw defiance. And I hungered for that defiance. I felt hunger deep and spiritual and sharp, in my mind and body, down in the fleshy arteries of my heart, and the eyes he threatened with seemed to gaze to no one but the song he sang, the hunger he felt.

> Yeah I know it's not so pretty
> Or so clean and pristine
> Buried somewhere underneath the rubble
> Of an American dream

Sometimes, though, the show was not what I thought it'd be. It was profane. And it would not redeem me. It would not redeem anything. Sometimes I would wake early in the morning before everyone else, and I would explore the town, and it would be bright, the air crisp, and I would wait for a glorious show that night to be the final act, the climax, the dénouement of my personal exploration and discovery. And the show would start, and it would go to shit.

On the road there was not verse one and two and then the chorus and then verse three and then the chorus and then a bridge and then an interlude and then another chorus. There was inconsistency. The crowd changed: their response, their receptivity, their patience, their blood-alcohol level. Even the Sixers changed. Though they never took the stage lightly, they changed. So many factors were at play one could not know anything.

What I valued changed, what was sacred to me.

Before "In Front of the World," Skunk told stories about his brother, for whom the song was written, stories about champagne corks popping into eyes, or stories about anniversaries spent at the Super 8 Motel, or about teeth being chipped by elbows at discos. Tonight in Virginia he told the story of the vibrators.

"I was like, 'Mom, I don't know,'" he was saying to the crowd.

After his brother had left for college, his mother had discovered two vibrators in his chest of drawers.

"'I don't know what to do, mom. I don't know.'"

He told other stories, sometimes, and they were all sacred to me, and I did not know why.

In the same way I remember this: Skunk and I were waiting in the van outside a record store in Seattle.

"Hey Skunk," I said, "could you pass me my shoes?"

He looked around, found them and held them up.

"These them?" he asked.

"Yes."

He proceeded to slowly roll down the window, lift my shoes and toss them onto the sidewalk. Outside Jessica was talking to the manager of the record store. They looked at us quizzically.

"Oh shit," Skunk said, and we laughed.

And this: On a night off we decided to go to *The Merry Wives of Windsor* at a small theater in rural Virginia. It was Stephen, Jessica and me, and we had stopped before the drive to get pizza. They ate in the car, and I drove. After I had parked the car I tried to eat my pizza, cold and soggy, in the time we had walking between the parking lot and the theater. I could not do it. Jessica wanted to get tickets with Stephen but Stephen said, "No, no, I'll wait here with Hunter," and with my cheeks bulging I smiled widely. On the drive back we recounted our favorite lines in our best British accents.

Skunk was the busiest of anyone. Not only was he the leader of the band musically and emotionally, but he was the CEO of what was Stephen Kellogg and the Sixers, Incorporated, and thus had daily conversations with agents, record executives, and other people in the industry. The times when he and I were alone were few, but on several occasions I caught glimpses of the Stephen past the business and even past the music.

He hated Hotel Aloft, a chain of hotels owned by the W. They were meant to be modern and chic. Their employees, tattooed and young, wore skinny jeans with skinny ties. They called elevators "lifts." In the lobby there was always a bar, usually with neon lights. Sometimes there was a pool table. In North Carolina, Stephen, Sam and I shared a room at one of these hotels. In the bathroom there was organic coffee and a copy of that week's GQ. The shower shared a wall with the bedroom; this wall was translucent, though not entirely transparent, glass. Sitting on the bed watching TV, Sam and I heard someone knock on the glass. It was Stephen in the shower. We turned around and saw—distorted by water, soap, glass, and dark hair—his pale ass.

Another time he and I had a shift together. The sun was rising. Four hours of sleep the night before had not been enough time for crust to form in the corners of our eyes.

As the sun rose, we drove east, into the bright light.

Outside the land was flat and blank, like a sheet of paper.

Skunk asked me questions: How are your folks? How is the tour? How are you?—how are you holding up?

What I wanted to say was that he had been right all along: The road was tough.

I was tired. I was dirty. I often felt alone. I felt useless. I was embarrassed.

By asking about me he had already given sufficient attention for me to know that he had been watching me, wondering about me, like a father who asks a question not so much for the answer, but for the weight of the question itself. It was all I needed to remember that though I often felt betrayed by that cinematic narrative of the road—*Almost Famous*, or books written about the road about drugs and groupies and revelry—that story was, sometimes, true. It was all I needed to remember those nights, moments before taking the stage, when Stephen caught my eye and smiled, when I saw the light in his eye like light playing off water, those nights when he and his band filled the entire room with the show, the show played for the sixty-five people in Fargo or the ninety-nine people in Houston or the one thousand in New York. On those nights there was nothing else.

And sometimes the Skunk I thought was the real Stephen and the Stephen on stage were the same.

In Champagne, Illinois, he said to Boots, Jessica, Kit, and me: "Let's have some fun."

We had slept together, driven together, eaten together. It was our second-to-last show.

He said, "Let's have some fun," and he meant it, because when the show started I saw he felt the warmth of alcohol, the boiler-maker in his coffee mug.

"So Goose came up to me and said, 'Hey Skunk, can you give me a thong?'"

He was telling a story into the microphone.

When they were young, the Sixers had sold thongs at shows. Now, they sold onesies. Skunk liked to joke that one thing had led to another.

In the story, Goose then said, "I'll meet you back at the hotel. I met this waitress. I think it's going somewhere."

At five in the morning he returned.

"Not so lucky," he told Skunk.

"Well," Skunk said, "what happened?"

"I gave her the thong, I bought her dinner, and I ate her out. Then she sent me home."

The crowd in Illinois laughed.

I stood beneath the exit sign. The colored lights above the stage were all streaming down like light through stained-glass windows in a church. The stage was dark, the venue full, a place of reverent awe and song and standing in between. And though the crowd that night was loud, he stayed them with his voice.

"At nineteen, he somehow found a rental car."

He was telling another story, and this story was about me.

"And we were on a bus," he continued, "the drives were long, but still he followed us."

He moved his hand in circles, pausing now.

"You want to write a book about us? Why? Why *us*? But he persisted."

Beneath the sign I stood and watched his eyes.

"We've spent the last three months with him," Skunk said, "and he's changed our lives," and then he plucked the strings of his guitar, notes soft and smooth and singing through the room, his eyes now shut, and soon he sang—

> Like a word from a murderous mouth
> News came to me, that I'd been too long South

The song turned over, first and second verse to calm before the chorus, Boots out front, the banjo in his hands, and Kit with bass, and Sam behind on pedal steel, a fluctuating ghost beneath the song, but all I saw were Stephen's eyes—

> I miss the innocence of purity
> I miss the things I never had
> I miss the way I used to be
> Before you ever got into my head

This was what I had wanted, had expected, had learned that others expected all along: New York City. This was the flawless show. This was our reward. It was Stephen's birthday. Technicians had been hired to record the show for a live album. There was no other way to end but with two sold-out nights at the Bowery Ballroom in New York City, New York. Tonight will be the climax, I thought. Tonight will be the night that redeems every vapid hotel room, every gray stretch of interstate, every moment of despair and loneliness—whether contrived or induced—I have felt on the road. This will be the consummation of my education.

Up a dark staircase was the dressing room, where friends and family members and record label executives dutifully visited the band before the show. There was a refrigerator with Red Stripe, soda, and a single bottle of Vitamin Water with Stephen's name taped to it. The walls were sponge-painted bronze. Several couches surrounded a table on which there were two bottles of wine and a bottle of Maker's Mark. Half-dressed, Stephen spoke with each person he saw, even if he only managed a brief acknowledgement. He smiled, thanked them for coming, shook their hand, promised them a hell of a show. Sam drank Amstel Light. He explained his first experience of touring with the Sixers as a member of the band; he had been inducted. Jessica sat with her husband. She was momentarily without a task, able to rest. Goose and Boots greeted other guests and friends. The voices filling the room created a primed hum. When the time came for it all to begin, Jessica evicted those who did not belong, leaving only the band and me.

"Hunter," Stephen said, looking over to me. I was standing with my pen and pad and watching. "Get in here." He motioned me to join. I had been watching but now I joined them in a huddle in the staircase, the stage just visible. The lights had been dimmed and the crowd could be heard. "This is it." This was it. This was the incantation with which the Sixers began each show. Each show they huddled as one and looked wildly to one another and then chanted "Leave your balls on the stage," louder and louder, "Leave your balls on the stage," working themselves into musical berserkers. I had always watched the ritual. And I had always wanted to join them but was afraid if I joined I would disrupt the liturgy. But now I was with them. And had been invited. And we looked at each other and we chanted the words, "Leave your balls on the stage," first slowly and no louder than one's voice in a conversation, then the pace increasing and the volume with it, "Leave your balls on the stage" again and again, faster until we no longer synchronized the words but overlapping they folded onto each other into a delirious mess until the cue came for the Sixers to start the show.

I was left watching, pen in hand.

They played "My Old Man"—harmonica and dobro—smoothly into the anthemic "Maria," and we—the audience, the band, me—knew where this was going. Everything was so beautifully scripted I couldn't believe it. I wondered how many encores the crowd would give them. I wondered if maybe the crowd wouldn't stop asking for more and more and the only reason the show would end was because the venue would kick us out. From where I stood I could see both the crowd and the band. They poured into each other energy and dynamics. It was all going splendidly and so I proposed a toast to myself. To all the tour has been, to all I have learned, to all I have done. I walked upstairs and poured myself a half-glass of Maker's Mark. I drank it off. I felt my nostrils and throat widen with heat. I took a Red Stripe from the refrigerator and returned to my usual spot.

Then Stephen's guitar stopped.

Someone went out onto the stage. We had triple-checked the batteries before the show. The Sixers stood. The music was stopped. It could not have been the batteries. Jessica stood beside me. Stephen said something into the microphone to the audience as Goose, standing behind him, tried to fix whatever was wrong. Jessica asked me to do something upstairs and I went upstairs and I drank another whiskey. Five minutes went by. I went back downstairs. The audience tried to laugh at whatever Stephen was saying. More lights had been turned on. It was strange all of us standing in the big room but there not being music. After ten minutes Sam and Boots played the guitar and drums to fill the emptiness. Then fifteen minutes. Then Stephen pronounced a spontaneous intermission and coolly walked off stage to tempered claps from the crowd. I was drunk. I told Jessica I had been drinking. She looked at me and said something. I was really very drunk and had not eaten much and had never been drunk before and was only one hundred and fifty pounds. I thought being drunk felt like being split inside yourself and one of you watching the other you and no masks and wondering if others knew you were drunk and wondering if you would say something silly and also feeling very odd physical sensations (I rubbed my neck) and all of it going slowly (Stephen walking from the stage toward Jessica and me) and then having conversations with yourself about what you were doing and how you were receiving what you yourself were doing. As soon as he was out of the audience's vision Stephen screamed and cursed and threw a bottle against the wall. Without a glance at Jessica or me he walked upstairs. A door slammed. Then I heard it open and him coming down the stairs. He stood in front of us, very close. "I can't do anything," he said, calmly at first and then raising his voice, his eyes brown and his hair brown and curly and his breath heavy and his face sweaty and contortedly twisted, "while my crew is acting like fucking cowards," and he stepped away, and I was wondering if I was part of this "crew" and was mildly happy if I was and then he turned around and looked straight at me and said, "You too, Hunter," and then I knew I was part of his crew but I did not feel happy. I was drinking another beer. After twenty minutes, or twenty-five or thirty minutes, the problem was fixed. I did not know what the problem was and I did not know who fixed it. The show was over and I was on one of the couches in the dressing room, lying down. I watched the after-show mingling. I wondered if anyone spoke about the break or if they acted as if nothing had happened. I saw everything from a different angle because I was lying down. I saw two blondes. One of them pointed at me. I was in the bathroom. I was throwing up. It was just liquid vomit, not much else. Goose brought me water. Boots brought me pita and hummus. Then he took a picture of me cradling the toilet. I was supposed to help Jessica pack the merchandise. I was supposed to help Kit load the trailer. I was supposed to help everyone clear the stage. None of those things I did. I did not even pack my own things. After vomiting I was carried to the van. It was November and I was in New York and it was cold. They went to the after-party and I curled myself into blankets in the van parked somewhere near the Bowery Ballroom and I wondered if I would spew more. I was not supposed to drink. When we finally left the city I was not supposed to open the door of the van as we sped along the highway—the highway with no shoulder, the van at full speed, New York City menacingly celestial against the night—and vomit.

When some time had passed and there were towns on which I could reflect I tried to understand my experience and how I had come to like this or that place or this or that person or this or that song or this or that arrangement. What I tried to learn was the old aphorism of the river not being the same river but still being water, which moved. I tried to answer the how. And when I learned to satisfy myself with an answer to the how then I tried to answer the why.

2

Boots

"THIS STORY CAN'T JUST be about Stephen's fucking kids!" Boots threatened in a mobster imitation of *The Godfather*. "This has got to translate to a movie."

"Yeah," Sam said, "yeah," mimicking the act. He stood behind me. Boots, in front, flipped his chair around and inched closer. He glared at me with his dark eyes.

"There's got to be something dramatic," he said.

Something was wrong with my story. This interrogation was the direct result of my botched interview that same morning with Brother Wease, the tattooed DJ during whose show—known for its "openness with listeners"—I offered memories of waking in a Smurf's blanket, happening upon Stephen in the kitchen wearing only boxer shorts, and playing princess with Sophia.

"Here's what I was thinking," Boots continued. "Russian roulette."

He described the opening of his film-to-be.

In a dark room with a single lamp—perhaps flickering—dangling from the ceiling, Boots, Sam and I sit around an old wooden table. Our shirts are torn. Maybe we have dust on our elbows, blood smeared on our cheeks, sweat on our brows. There's a bottle of whiskey. A broken fan. And Venetian blinds.

Sam holds the revolver. He looks at us intently, spins the cylinder, lifts the gun, and pulls the trigger.

No bullet. He hands it to me.

Spin, lift, pull.

No bullet. Then Boots.

Spin, lift, pull.

Cut to the first show.

My first Sixers show had been in the late spring of that year in Columbus, Ohio. I remember nothing of the music except that in a vague way it seemed exceptional. What I remember most poignantly is watching the Sixers play and hearing them but being preoccupied with whether or not I was bobbing my head in a suave manner, with the composition I had created between my shoes, plum- and aqua-colored, and my jacket, a faintly pinstriped blazer. I remember they played "4th of July" and I remember they looked like what you thought rock stars should look like: sweaty, bearded, signing autographs.

Boots, I saw, was wearing green Chuck Taylors of the exact same style as mine. Waiting for the line of fans and new fans to recede, I grew excited about our serendipitously shared sense of style. I felt like a masquerader with my planned wardrobe, but now it was paying dividends. At this stage of my dubious debut I needed anything I could get. I was nothing to the Sixers and I knew it, knew I could offer nothing to invigorate what might have been perceived as the sputtering, spiraling descent of a band too talented and true for the charts. That was how I had learned to see them. I was no market value. I knew that. But the shoes. I had to hope in the shoes.

I was introduced to Boots. He smiled very moderately. In fact he looked quite suspicious of me. He was not impressed. Maybe he had not noticed the shoes on our feet. Maybe I should have told him I dabbled in percussion while in high school. His beard, I saw, grew mostly on the sides of his face, and while he did have a thin and dark mustache, he lacked the little roads of hair that connect the mustache with the rest of the beard. All in all it gave him a more advanced version of my own threadbare facial hair. He went back to the dressing room and we exchanged no further words that night.

Before my trip to Columbus the video blogs I had watched gave me, in a three-times-removed sort of way, a sense that I already knew the band. I had gathered some information on each member. Boots, drummer for the Sixers, graduated film major from the University of Massachusetts, and wearer of t-shirts, fedoras, and his beard, is the host of these films.

"So," he says to Jessica who, in this episode, is the interviewee. "You said you're related to Stephen Kellogg of Stephen Kellogg and the Sixers." In this particular series he is sorting facts from fiction for the viewer, profiling each member of the band—Stephen, Sam, Kit—and Jessica, their tour manager. Having already established that Stephen is neither the popular children's author of the same name nor related to the cereal manufacturer, he now asks Jessica about the shared name "Kellogg."

"Are you married to him?" he asks.

"No, no," she says. "We're not married, Boots. We're first cousins."

In another, the camera opens with Kit, Stephen and Boots sitting side by side by side, all wearing hooded sweatshirts, all wearing fedoras, talking about the road. Boots asks about the shows, and after saying a few generic things regarding the great venues and lively crowds, Stephen says, "One of the things I'm doing on the side in this tour, which I daresay I'm even more excited about, is—uh—is Handy and Candy."

Handy is Stephen's right hand. Candy, his left.

"I make movies," he explains, "with Handy and Candy."

Boots concludes the interview by saying, with an unwaveringly expressionless face, "I think it's great for fans to see what you do in your spare time."

Art, I had always believed, was sovereign. And being an Artist, I thought, was not so much an occupation as it was a calling. A calling to be approached with reverence. With silence. I thought the Artist, more than any man, bears the burden of being, and if this was the case these people, I thought, could not be artists. I laughed at the antics I saw in their films but I was repulsed. In nine episodes—episodes I had watched and watched again—I had seen the Sixers with slicked-back hair singing "Little Deuce Coupe" in a hotel room, I had seen a dirty sock puppet and a tuba in Home Depot and a penis whistle in a gag shop, I had heard a story involving Internet dating and Tourette's syndrome, I had heard the

opening music of *Star Wars*, and I had also heard Stephen ask the question, of his own song, as he walked onto the stage, "How does this start again?" and I had seen nothing reverent, and the things that were sovereign were only ephemerally sovereign, having in them no trace of permanence, nothing weighty or powerful, and the whole vocation, the Artistic calling with which they had been blessed, was spent uselessly—William Carlos Williams writing greeting cards.

The throng flowed steadily in Grand Central Station. There were businessmen, businesswomen, and cleaning crews erecting CAUTION: WET FLOORS signs. There were homeless people playing rhythms on upturned buckets. There were tourists with disposable cameras, cashiers at newsstands and people with their necks craned up to the large sign that flashed the departure times, tracks, and destinations of the trains. There were people standing with food, people walking with food, and people stuffing food in their bags. People whispering, people talking, people calling out loudly. People looking happy, people looking sad, people looking anxious. People walking, people jogging, people running. There was leaving and there was connecting and there was arriving.

I navigated the mob, pulling my suitcase and carrying my backpack. On the road I always carried my backpack. I carried empty notebooks and I carried notebooks I had filled completely but wanted with me in case I needed to reference them. And I did not want to lose them and was wary of leaving them in my suitcase. The notebooks became the book I was supposed to be writing. I carried a Bible. I carried pens, but not pencils. I carried the 1957 copy of *A Farewell to Arms* I purchased in Annapolis. I sometimes carried my computer. I carried my phone and my wallet and I always carried either a sweater or my black bomber jacket. I did not like to be unprepared for a drastic change in temperature. This happened often and was always unexpected, snow or desert or mountains or plains or wind or humidity. Twelve hours in a van could change the climate, and if sometimes you lost track, or lost the will to keep track, of where you were going, as I did, then you woke up and were, without prior notice, very cold or very hot. I carried so many things I gave the impression of a vagrant. Finally I saw Boots. He was now beardless, freshly shaved for the new tour, and his brown fedora looked new. He too pulled a rolling suitcase and carried a snare drum in a soft black case and a backpack.

We were rendezvousing in New York for the beginning of the tour. It was September. We would take a train from Grand Central Station to Connecticut, where the rest of the band waited our arrival. That night there would be a rehearsal and the next day we were to begin. We walked to the platform with our things.

The things we carried on our backs and in the trailer were, for the most part, determined by necessity. We carried guitars, electric and acoustic. We carried keyboards. We carried amps and microphones and stands. We carried pedals. We carried remote earpieces through which the Sixers, during the show, heard each other's instruments. We carried the banjo, the tuba, the mandolin. We carried an accordion. We carried Pam the Printer and Allen the Table, the small, knee-high table onto which Stephen, during the show, set his harmonicas and, sometimes, his whiskey; we carried the harmonicas in a military-grade black case. We carried boxes of shirts, and boxes filled with smaller boxes of CDs. We pinned the shirts onto black grates, long and heavy, hard to carry. The type of show we were to play mandated what specific instruments we extracted from the trailer. If we were playing a full concert we carried everything. From the trailer—usually parked within fifty feet of the open doors of the venue, but sometimes farther away—to the stage. Sometimes in rain, sometimes in snow, sometimes wet with sweat. Sometimes up a staircase or through only a single door. Sometimes up an elevator. If, however, we were playing three to five songs at a book or record store, we carried only one or two instruments per Sixer, almost always acoustic. If we were playing a radio station it was the same except that there might be even less space. Sometimes it was only Stephen playing his guitar. Sometimes Stephen, Sam and Kit had instruments while Boots shook egg shakers.

We carried things we did not need: pillows, blankets sewn by our moms, photographs of our children, books and unused bottles of wine, whiskey, or vodka, since the Sixers, at least that fall, rarely drank more than a beer or two any given night. We carried trail mix and we always carried—this we did need—water.

Boots and I shook hands. I followed him to the ticket machines and tried to purchase my own ticket, but he, being a native New Yorker and having purchased his in seconds, commandeered my machine. I watched his hand swiping the screen. A piece of paper popped out, I took it, and we found a compartment on the train.

I looked down at my ticket and saw the words THIS IS NOT A TICKET in red letters. It was the receipt.

I said, "Uh, Boots." I showed it to him and I said, "What should I do?"

He looked at me.

I knew I had to buy another ticket in the several minutes before our scheduled departure. I walked slowly out of the compartment, rounded a corner, and as soon as I was sure Boots could no longer see me I sprinted to the ticket machine once again. Someone had already taken my ticket so I bought another, returned to the compartment, heard the whistle of the conductor, felt the quick jerking start of the train, and watched the world go by outside the window.

Several shows into the tour I noticed a phenomenon regarding Boots and me that would continue throughout our time together. Perhaps it should not have been so surprising that, despite the sharp looks of disapproval I thought he gave me, at least in the beginning, we were forged of the same stuff. After all, we purchased the same sneakers. We grew the same beard. We were both drummers. Neither of us did much in the van. Others wrote emails or read books or returned calls, but Boots and I, we slept. Sometimes we listened to music. Thus I should not have been surprised to find shortly into the tour that, despite whatever apprehension he felt about me joining the troupe, and despite my fear of him, and despite our very little verbal communication, there surfaced a certain palpable bond between us, something deeper and more transcendent than our simple shared sense of style: our taste in women.

I remember the first time it happened. Standing by the stage moments before the show began, I examined the lighted faces of the women in the crowd. We were in Minneapolis, and Minneapolis, I thought, topped the list I had recently started of the most beautiful cities in the United States. My hands rested on a guitar case as I looked from left to right across the Scandinavian-descended collection of beauties. I was clearly, I thought, part of the band. My ALL ACCESS laminate dangled below my neck, my face was unshaven for several days, my jeans were skinny and rolled-up and I wore my brightly colored Chuck Taylors. All of this, supported by the fact that I stood on the side of the musician, the side on which those people were not allowed, loudly suggested I was in some way part of this act.

Then I caught sight of a girl in a blue dress. My eyes stopped. I had found what I was looking for. About my age, blonde hair like a waterfall sparkling in the sun falling down over her supply curved shoulders, her dress blue like the sea against her incandescently golden skin. She caught me looking. I blushed and retreated my eyes.

While the Sixers played we made eye contact several more times, this beautiful girl and me, and that was excitement enough. Her eyes froze me solid with fear and I, of course, said absolutely nothing to her, despite what might have been construed as an invitation.

The show ended, the crowd dissipated and thoughts of making sweet love to a thin blonde filled my imagination. No longer was my post-show routine a routine. Oh tasteful darling! I imagined her. Happily and wholeheartedly I placed the curvy guitars into their cases, fitting like keys into keyholes, snug and tight. Happily I turned on and off what needed to be turned on and off.

I went back to the dressing room to continue packing and there, sitting next to Boots, sitting snugly and warmly next to Boots, was the girl in the blue dress.

She looked at me, and I looked at her. I thought I saw her smirk. She knew. And I knew.

I could not turn around, so I dropped to my hands and knees and unplugged the power cord that went to the printer. My last duty of the night.

Later she and Boots made out in the parking lot.

In Atlanta three tall and leggy belles eyed me during the show. I thought about it. I knew it was greedily ambitious of me, and mostly evidence of the power of the imagination, and of course I said nothing, and of course I found them backstage after the show talking with Boots. He went home with one of them and the next morning, all six of us sitting in the van, someone asked him, "Did you bone her?"

The formula was easy to memorize: I see girl, girl sees me, girl chooses Boots. My position with the band, it seemed, was high enough to win me eyes, but too low to win me more. So I looked and looked and never spoke or acted. I was a coward, lowly and common, the rotting soil of the earth, and Boots was a hero, proud and victorious, confident in all his exploits. We gradually recognized our mutual attraction to the same type of woman and it became a fascinating headline on the road, but in St. Louis I had a chance to rewrite the traditional script.

I had been instructed to work the merchandise table. I was no salesman but I sat faithfully, if smugly, bored and a little frustrated, full of self-pity, and then like a vision she danced across the smooth wooden floor of the venue as the house music played overhead. She had short dark hair, and a short dark dress. She wasn't a beauty, but she was more than all right for me. The space between us was empty but full of my thoughts.

She looked at the t-shirts. Looked at me. Smiled.

And after giving the sales pitch I had been given to give, I stumbled over my words and started talking to her. I was quick to clarify that I was traveling with the band and that this—this lowly duty of working the economics—was in no way indicative of my position, and in fact it was a rarity. I, I told her, was a writer. Oh, a writer? Yes, yes (very casually). I'm writing a book. Oh!

The depth of our conversation was like the sea, the emotional poignancy like *The Titanic*.

Moments after the show I stood on stage and scoured the crowd. I saw her. There was no turning back, because I had made up my mind to talk to her, to not allow a formula to reign over me.

Some stories, though, maybe were formulas.

There she was with Boots.

I rushed to the dressing room.

"See!" I pleaded to the others. "It happens every time."

"Come on," they said, "what is it?"

"It's Boots."

In California I had one last opportunity.

Crouching in a stairwell to the side of the stage, I watched the show. The Sixers were playing well under poor circumstances, as they often did, and I was soaking up the music. The relative beauty of the crowd had not even entered my mind, had not entered my mind until out of the darkness a woman walked up the stairs, stood close by, and peered over my shoulder, looking at the set list in my hands. She asked, "Is that what they're playing?"

She was a woman, not a girl.

She wore tall boots, a short purple dress, and a yellow scarf. Her hair was dirty-blonde. She did not wear makeup.

"Oh," I said, surprised, "yeah."

"Oh!" she exclaimed excitedly. "That's my favorite one!"

She reached her hand over me and, grazing my shoulder, pointed to a song on the list.

"Cool, cool," I said, coolly trying to play it cool.

Her name was Cassandra.

Throughout the Sixers' set we spoke, loudly during anthems and softly during ballads. She loved animals; she saved stray dogs and manatees. She had graduated from college in Maine and had lived here, in San Francisco, for about six years. In my head I tried to work out how old she was, tried to do the math. At least twenty-eight, I deduced.

"I'm a writer," I said very loudly. "I'm writing a book."

She left after our pleasant conversation. She said she wasn't sure if she would stay for the entire show. She said maybe she would.

When we had packed up everything, leaving the stage ready for Tyrone Wells, the headliner, I frantically roamed the venue for Cassandra, the woman of at least twenty-eight years who was from Maine and rescued manatees.

I saw her, standing alone, phone in hand, in queenly purple.

I said to me, Don't be a fucking coward.

"So you decided to stay for the show?" I yelled over the music.

She looked up and said hello.

We talked and talked. We stood very near each other. I was thrilled. I could perhaps smell the alcohol on her breath. I felt her breath, smelled her perfume. As we spoke she drew closer and as she drew closer—presumably to hear me better—she pressed her chest against my arm, now tucked tightly between her breasts.

Downstairs, she wanted to share some music with me. I said okay.

She said, "Email or text?

"Text."

She saved my number in her phone, my pocket vibrated, and just as this was happening, Boots walked by. He arched his eyebrows, looked at me, and smiled.

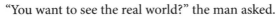

"You want to see the real world?" the man asked.

Boots and I stood in a parking lot waiting for the others to get out of the van when a security guard, old but thick and strong, had emerged from a small shelter in the center of the lot. He was smoking a cigarette. He spoke with a thick Eastern European accent and now stood with Boots and me. When he moved his body it did not seem like he was old. We started walking away from him but he walked with us. We had almost reached the end of the lot.

I looked at Boots and Boots looked at me.

"You want to see the real world?" the man asked.

"Excuse me?" Boots asked for us.

"You want to see the real world?" he repeated for a third time. "Yes," now exhaling smoke, "North Milwaukee—that's the real world."

We said nothing.

"Shooting all the time," he said somberly. Then, abruptly, "Bang!" waving his cigarette around, the butt glowing fiery orange. "Bang! Bang!"

He told us he was from Serbia. He had done high-level security here in Milwaukee for a number of years before the parking lot job, remembering in particular an Usher concert at which, he claimed, he was the only Caucasian. He had fought the Taliban in Afghanistan.

Boots started calling me "son," so I started calling him "dad." I have no recollection of the specific circumstances surrounding this affectionate nomenclature, but it happened and we went with it. Son, he would say, Could you grab my banjo? or Son, this is how you do it or Son, you're doing that wrong and I would say Hey Dad, or I would say, Hey, Dad, what are you listening to? or I would say, What should I say to this girl?

In Indianapolis a girl I knew—a girl I wanted to impress—came to the show.

I saw her across the street. She looked lovely. She had big, honey-brown eyes and wore a coat over a cream-colored top and dark jeans. We were to have dinner and then watch the Sixers. It was almost a date. I had known her since the third grade and had wooed her since the fifth, when, for Valentine's Day, I filled a small white box with Reese's Peanut Butter Cups and dollar bills.

I colored the box pink with a highlighter while our teacher read aloud *The Hobbit*. At the time I didn't know her dad owned an oil company. Nicole was the type of girl who, on a whim, because there was nothing better to do, decided to work on a farm on a remote island. She had danced in New York City for a ballet company but was also interested in arts management. It was all very attractive. And very intimidating.

After saying hello we found the only restaurant in the area, a Mexican cantina. We were in Fountain Square outside of downtown Indianapolis; it was a post-war bloom collection of rusting signs, blank marquees and buildings with no signs at all. Outside it was windy and cold. Inside, the walls were painted with desert scenes and trimmed with terra-cotta.

As Nicole and I were sitting down, the waitress arriving with chips and salsa, Boots walked through the front door with Jon McLaughlin, an Indiana native, a singer and piano player, a friend of the Sixers who would, later that night, sit in on their set.

"Hey Dad," I said, trying to get his attention.

Boots looked over and smiled.

"Well look who it is!" he said. He was pleasantly surprised. He and Jon came over and sat with us, Jon by Nicole, Boots by me. Introductions were made. I shook Jon's hand. He had brown shaggy hair and was boyishly handsome.

"Great to meet you," Boots said to Nicole. "So how do you know this kid?" He nudged my arm.

I watched them shake hands.

It was strange, watching their hands, their skin touching: the convergence of my old life—Dallas, high school, even the prepubescent years—and the road—whoever I was now, whoever I was becoming. It was a struggle to know how to reconcile them.

In California the worst thing that could happen to a touring band—other than a drug-induced death—happened. I discovered it when, as I settled into my seat in the van, Stephen tapped my shoulder and held up a notepad on which there was a scribbled message: "I'm sick." So sick, in fact, that he was physically incapable of speaking. So sick he would fly home that night. Stephen was, of course, the lead singer, the rhythm guitar player, and the frontman. He told the jokes and he told the stories. When an agent or executive called, he answered. When someone asked a question, he responded. He was the emotional leader as well as the vocal leader. He ordered the set, he critiqued the show, he praised, he arranged, and he roused and rallied his troupe. They were his men, every night. But now he was gone. Could do nothing.

The Sixers spoke back and forth. It was now a democracy. The first order of business was to decide whether or not to play the show that night. All reason said there was no reason to play. It was Sunday night, the Sixers had never before played Sacramento, and they were opening for Tyrone Wells. There was a fair chance that not one single person would be there to see them. The financial gain to be had was minimal. And none of these facts took into account that the Sixers, in the span of a few hours, would have to learn, rehearse, and play a full set of music as they never had before. When the discussion started I was silently hoping that they'd cancel the show. I was tired. We were all tired. And we all knew that a night off might benefit us more than walking in stark naked to a show for people who had never even heard of the band. But when the decision was reached—the decision to play without Stephen—I realized that not only would the show be a rich source of hilarity—this was sure—but it would be the point in the script at which there was no recycled narrative, no template. In other words, U2 didn't play a show if Bono couldn't speak.

What happened was this: The stuffy air inside the van changed. Sam, Kit and Boots spoke up. They jotted things down, posed questions, composed the show from scratch. They were discussing how to play the single off the album, "Shady Esperanto and the Young Hearts."

Kit, while driving the van, looking in the rearview mirror to the others: "Which verse do you want, Boots?"

Boots, thinking quickly: "I'll take the first."

Kit: "Do you think you could take the third as well?"

Boots: "Yeah. And I'll stick with my same harmonies. Sam, do you know the harmony on that?"

Sam, making a face: "Not sure . . . is it this?" He sang a note.

Boots, nodding: "Yes!"

They decided to split up the lead vocals, sometimes by song and sometimes by verses within a song. They decided instruments, arrangements on stage, order of the songs, and who'd do the talking. The new voice of the band was Boots.

Before the show we stopped at a bookstore to play a fifteen-minute set. Kit and Boots sang the lead vocals while Sam played guitar. In between songs Stephen, who was also playing guitar, wrote messages on his notepad which he handed to Boots, who then read them aloud to the six vaguely interested people sitting scattered among the thirty or so chairs. "Sacramento," Boots read, "I am sorry to inform you, but I am sick." While Boots read, Stephen hopped around making facial expressions of sadness, happiness, excitement. "But my band is here to save the day!" Then they sang another song.

They produced the show. And you would not have guessed that they produced it in a bookstore in suburban California. It could have been a football stadium. And you would not have guessed that the crowd for whom they played was six people who had probably never heard of them in the first place and who would probably never listen to them again.

That night I took a walk while the Sixers, without Stephen, who was already asleep at the hotel, rehearsed with the miniature guitar in the van. It was Sunday evening. Shops and restaurants were closed, the streets dark and empty. I walked several blocks in each direction, looking for coffee. I couldn't find anything but enjoyed the walking. Alone, carrying my backpack, I often wandered the towns. It was ecstasy on the road, a time away from the static of the van, the impersonal of the hotel, the mayhem of the venue. Of course those things were not always predictable, not always static or impersonal or filled with mayhem, and the van could at times be restful, the hotels charming, the venues electric, but they were always public. There was no or very little retreat. So I walked and walked. Sometimes I would wake early if we had already arrived in whatever town we were playing in, and I would use public transportation, or I would walk, and I would explore that town. It was respite. However peripheral and limited my explorations were, because of time, because of money, because of my own changing mood any given day, I always developed some sensibility about any place, some affection or, perhaps, malignance. Fargo, I told people, was cold. I hypothesized that perhaps its isolation in the gray unknown of the country produced in its locals a harshness. I was particularly fond of Northampton, Massachusetts, and Bozeman, Montana. My relationship with Carrboro, North Carolina, was deep but complicated. But the more I traveled the more I saw how vain or unpredictable any hypothesis was. In Carrboro I befriended a fascinating bus driver and then felt, later that night, completely abandoned. In Northampton I was staying with friends, and I was well rested, and I was told where to go. In Bozeman I woke to mountains and, at the co-op, saw a beautiful woman. In Fargo I felt inexplicably lonely. These are meant to be circumstances, or suggestions as to the variables involved, not explanations; there was not always an explanation. The only explanation was that it would be different every time, that to wrap something up was to kill it. The variables always changed, and they themselves were always changing.

That was the road. The more I saw, the more there was to see, the more to know. Every town, every street, every lamppost moved. I, too, moved, and kept moving. Everything was part of a systematic increase of motion, systematic I knew not how, but did see, an increase that could evoke the deepest empathy and intimacy with those I met on buses, at venues, and most deeply and often with the Sixers, but an increase that could also evoke the most poignant and realized loneliness.

I was approached on the empty and dark streets by a man, neither young nor old, wearing blue jeans and a t-shirt.

"Hello, sir," he said to me. He smiled kindly. He walked up hesitantly and said again, "Hello, sir."

I said nothing.

Then he said, "Would you like something to eat?"

He extended his hands. In them he held a plate of food. He thought I was poor; he thought I was homeless. Behind him I saw a van and a number of others in jeans and shirts standing in an assembly line, making these plates of food. When a plate was created, one of them would take it and wander until they found someone homeless. I saw a few around.

"I'm not hungry," I said.

"Are you sure?" he asked. He extended his arms, moving the plate—but not himself—a little closer.

I walked away, then saw a coffee shop. It was closed. By the door stood a woman with a grocery cart of blankets and food. Her home. I tried the door even though no one was inside.

"There's food over there," she said.

"I'm not hungry," I said again, and returned to the venue.

The lights of the stage shone to Sam, Boots and Kit. They sang "The Bear" and "Shady Esperanto" and "The Apartment Song" by Tom Petty. They laughed and forgot lines and wore jeans and shirts and fedoras. Boots conducted the interactions with the crowd. The crowd adored him. His jokes were flawless composites of cynicism and wit. I watched from the side of the venue. I had never seen a crowd take so many pictures and I hadn't seen Boots laugh so much. He explained that Stephen was sick but, what the hell, this was a Sunday night in Sacramento, California, and they weren't going to leave the people without music. He joked and his jokes hit their marks. Sam dropped to his knees, played the guitar on his back, and laid down and continued his solo. Kit stripped down to his underwear. They unplugged, Boots and his banjo directing the quieting of the stage.

All this they did on a Sunday night in a rundown, shutdown part of Sacramento in a club in the basement of the building that they—Boots, Sam, Kit—changed from insipid to teeming. They did this for fewer than two hundred people, most of whom—maybe all of whom—were there to see the other band.

And I wondered why.

I was never myself around Boots because I was constantly afraid of him, constantly aware that his position in the band was the master of style, of suavity. Stephen always told me that Boots was the most urbane person in the band, the person around whom you yourself felt, at once, untouchably elevated and utterly worthless, elevated by association, worthless by comparison, and since I had not spent the many years it apparently required to earn the elevation by association, I spent my time in mock silence and silent fear, in admiration of Boots. Once in a clothing store in Michigan, I walked around inspecting shirts with Boots, or near Boots. I kept my eyes on the shirts but watched him. He wore Nike sneakers and dark jeans and he liked the Mets. Mets fans were always mysterious and they possessed patience, or perhaps begrudging tolerance. He was from New York. He was Jewish. He lived in Brooklyn now, alone, near Polish immigrants who still spoke Polish. He knew the differences between Martin Scorsese's *No Direction Home* and D.A. Pennebaker's *Don't Look Back*, documentaries on Bob Dylan. His favorite band was Pearl Jam. He drank too much coffee. He made and recorded his own music in addition to that of the Sixers. He was single. He was hesitant. He once wore a purple banana suit during a show in which the Sixers covered a Prince album. He did not particularly like to be photographed; I always had my camera with me. When he had time, he slept. He slept and slept. He was quietly mysterious and when we left the clothing store and went to the van to wait for the others, we waited wordlessly.

Then, in Iowa, after the show, in the van, I made a speech.

The night was cool and dark. That was the night my friends had come to the show, the night Stephen had brought me onto the stage, the night of my return to the state of Iowa. We were parked in an empty parking lot. My friends had gone, the road had returned, and I knew I had to say something to the band because I had been afraid. I had been afraid because they were new and so was the road and I had been silent for fear and I had not been myself, and I hated sentimentality and I hated that I was a sentimental person afraid of himself, and I hated the feeling that I would say something silly or unimportant. I was the youngest and I did nothing of worth and I hid behind the persona of a writer, but I didn't write, had never written, and it was something only to say to people who asked why, who asked why I was on the road and I said, or Stephen said, or Jessica said, a writer, vain words, so I wondered why they tolerated me.

I started but my voice was shaky, my throat quivering, dry, and I said I wanted to say something, and I said, "Thank you," said, "Thank you for letting me be here on the road thank you and even if the crowd is shit as they were tonight I'm here, I'm always here on the side of the stage loving your music, loving every measure." I said other things and then I shut myself up. I had made a speech and maybe I had embarrassed myself—I felt embarrassed—but I needed to.

Boots, sitting in the bench behind me, reached his arm over the seat and rested his hand on my shoulder.

I performed my most courageous feat on the road one night in Seattle in the middle of my most mundane routine: packing the trailer. I performed the liturgy of opening the trailer doors, pulling out the suitcases, propping the doors open with the suitcases, and waiting for the others to begin bringing amps and instruments. I set a case of water down on top of a bag and then I saw a hand swiftly and suddenly slither its way around the door and into the case, taking a bottle of our water.

I stepped out onto the sidewalk to see the perpetrator already opening his stolen prize.

"Hey, buddy," I said. "Is that yours?"

He turned around.

At five feet eleven inches, under one hundred and fifty pounds, I am not the most intimidating figure, but, I thought, I am wearing my bomber jacket, which adds a visual fifteen to twenty pounds, and I am wearing my torn-and-tattered gray pants, which perhaps suggest a certain *Max Payne* ruggedness.

The theft walked toward me, his steps askew, his weight forward over his toes.

"Sorry," he said, "sorry." He got a little closer. "I'll—I'll give you a dollar." He reached into his pocket for his wallet.

My eyes had not left his. He stood about six feet away.

"I don't want a dollar," I said. "Don't take things that aren't yours, okay pal?"

By now Kit and Boots had stumbled onto the scene and were watching.

"It's okay," Boots said to him, "just get going."

He left.

Boots turned to me.

"I got a kick out of that," he said, "you were a totally different guy."

The sky was sun-scorched pink. The clouds held leases on the light, pulsing purple and orange, stretching with the horizon. The sky was a system of color sensations. The land itself breathed back, the trees and brush embracing green against the coming winter, the grass a fading yellow on the hills. We moved across the land. We wanted home. The West is lonely, we said, for New Englanders. This was wilderness. This was barren land. What was for us here? We watched the mountains. Ahead the road curved out of sight. The plots of land divided the earth into slightly varied planes of color, like a map of Africa. I was not lonelier than I was when the sun set in Montana and the vast and profound wilderness fled to darkness. The darkness was an empty canvas onto which I painted myself. I remember that I was not lonelier and I remember that Boots asked me if I was all right and I remember that the loneliness did not go away, of course, but I remember it changed. I missed my home; we all did. The movement sapped our strength. It thinned our hair and stretched our spirits thin. I remember the solicitude with which we drove across the western portion of Montana. The sun fell and we hungered, we thirsted. We found the Montana Bar and Grill. The grill is off, said the bartender, but I can fire up the fryer in less than ten. He wore a baseball cap. His beard was thick, his eyes brown like soil. We want chicken strips, we all said. Mounted on the walls were the severed heads of deer and bucks and bears and guinea fowl. The floors and ceilings were beams of polished wood. We watched a man and woman at the pinball machine. He was drunk. He pushed her around. We exchanged nervous glances, we watched TV, and then we ate our chicken strips. In the morning we woke with the sun streaming to us from the east.

Brooklyn was the end of my journey. The tour was over. I would fly from New York to Texas and it would be over.

I stayed with Boots.

We watched *Hot Rod*. We watched *The Squid and the Whale*. We watched *Arrested Development* and we ordered Chinese food and we walked to a diner. We ordered chocolate-chip pancakes and a peppered-turkey sandwich. We ate. We went on the town. We consulted each other on what to wear. We were meeting three young ladies at a bar called Matchless. I was of course not yet twenty-one, but we had the whole thing staged and prepared beforehand. I was nervous and Boots asked me more than once if I was all right and if I would go through with it.

We approached the bar and I saw the bouncer sitting on a stool by the door.

When we were close and Boots was pulling out his wallet he said to me so the bouncer could hear, "Oh you forgot your ID didn't you?"

"Oh yeah," I said, looking from the bouncer to Boots. I pressed my pockets as if I had no idea where my ID could have been. "Shit."

"How old are you?" the bouncer asked me.

Very quietly, "Twenty."

I couldn't lie.

Boots looked shocked and I felt very awful about telling the truth.

"What'd he say?" the bouncer asked Boots.

"He said twenty."

"I can't let you in," the bouncer said.

We stepped away for a moment and deliberated.

"Dude," Boots said. "I can't believe you! Are you fucking kidding me?"

"I'm sorry."

"Dude. You just need to be *okay* with lying to a bar."

"Okay."

We sat in silence until I saw two of the girls talking to the bouncer, pleading with him, grabbing at his wrists and pointing to me. I saw one open her wallet and say, "How much?"

It only took ten dollars to get me in.

I didn't know anything but the things that stayed with me. I thought I was in control of them but of course I wasn't. Sometimes I tried to contrive what I would remember and what, I thought, would eventually go into the book. I'd think to myself about a certain show or event or night, This will be an important moment. And then—almost inevitably—I remembered nothing particular about the night at all.

3

Cousin

I FIRST EMAILED STEPHEN Kellogg and the Sixers on an April morning the spring before. I wrote that I was a writer. I was a freshman in college and pleaded with them saying, "I'm in college and college sucks!" I asked for their empathy: "Ya know?" And following the announcement that I would be a prime candidate for writing a fine book about their band, and in relation to my loathing for school, I posed what I thought was an apt question, a question I unknowingly wrote with painfully wrong grammar: "Why should writer's go to school?" When, two hours later, my inbox chimed, it was Jessica who responded.

She signed her email, "Tour manager and protective as hell." I was nervous. She'd responded but it wasn't particularly cordial. She wrote, of my proposition that I join the Sixers on the road, "I can't say I'm wowed by the style of your solicitation." And also, "Hell, I can't tell if you understand the band even a little," citing the lack of "seriousness" in my pitch, the absence of "class." In the end, though, she told me, "I'm not going to forward this to the band just yet, but"—she conceded finally—"you've got some balls."

A month later I was in Ohio. It was my first time meeting the band in person. Somehow I had convinced them—by sending samples of a high school blog and a short story about a woman whose grandfather died—that I was not such a bad writer after all. Wearing black jeans, a white v-neck, a lightly pinstriped blazer and a yellow baseball cap pulled backward, I paced in a garden. My shoes were colored aqua and plum. I tried to evoke the image of a writer who was also a cool, sociable guy, the sort of guy you wouldn't mind having around as a friend at a bar or cocktail party. I was pacing the garden because I had arrived two full hours early. I called Jessica, she answered, and she said they were not ready for me yet.

I sat in a restaurant alone while I waited. I ordered salmon, which I did not even like. Waiting for the food, I took the proposal I had written out of my breast-pocket. It explained why this—taking me on the road to write a book—was such a tremendously good idea. The first section, "The Idea," explained the intelligence of taking an underage person who had only just left home in Texas for school in Iowa on tour across the entirety of the continental United States of America; it was intelligent because, I argued, it was a unique thing to do. "What It Could Do" was the next section; it enlightened the band (who was signed with a label and had agents who did booking and promoting) to what a potentially genius marketing scheme this could be. All in all, my proposal was edgy—I had used the word "fucking"—and it was literary—there were four dashes, three semicolons, two colons—and it was absolutely revolutionary—"This hasn't been done before," I'd claimed. I had used Roman numerals and I had inserted a table and I had used the word "idealistic."

When I finished dinner and called Jessica again, she said they were running late, so I paced more and finally made it to the venue. She looked tired and said, "I could have planned this months ago and it still would have gone to shit."

There were t-shirts pinned on the wall behind her, CDs on a table in front of her. She wore glasses and had a mass of brown curly hair. A keychain and an ALL ACCESS pass rattled against her hip, clipped through a loop of her jeans by a carabineer.

"How's your trip been so far?" she asked.

The day before, I had driven from Iowa City to Cedar Rapids, then had flown from Cedar Rapids to Chicago, and from Chicago to Columbus, where I had been picked up by a friend of my mom's, who had driven me to her son's apartment, in the living room of which, on the couch, I had slept.

"Great," I said, "Columbus is cool. Yeah, it's a cool town. Have y'all played here before?"

"Yeah."

"Cool, cool."

"Hey," she said, pulling up a chair, "come sit, I need to stand anyway."

And I sat. I said thank you and sat on that side of the table and, instead of shirts and CDs, I saw the concert-goers, happy and loud and drinking beers in cups that, as Jessica noted, looked like to-go containers for generous portions of Thai food. The view had changed.

As I sat with Jessica I had the feeling I was already being evaluated. I tried to sound intelligent. Somehow we had started talking about art, something I knew only cursory facts about. When she started to describe her favorite painting—in which a peasant girl gazing at the viewer holds a scythe, her feet bare, her eyes tired, her dress plain, the colors in the surrounding landscape muted greens and grays and browns—I, in the interest of the worldly air I was attempting to affect, suddenly fearing it would be impolite to interrupt her description, and hoping to construct an agreeable impression of myself, feigned acquaintance with the artist, a man named William Bouguereau. I said something about Paul Cézanne because he was a painter I liked and he was French.

Looking at the time she said, "I've got to go get the guys on stage. Can you stay here?"

I understood this to be a command rather than a question I could answer, and I stayed.

And then it was summer. In Columbus the band had said to stay in touch and we would try to arrange a time when I could join them for a few days, as a sort of trial run, another step to see if I was fit for the coast-to-coast tour that fall. The whole summer I anticipated an absolute and resounding *no* from the band, but it never came. I was a counselor at a camp where I could only check my phone and email on the weekends, and so one Saturday evening as I spoke with Jessica on the phone, as I paced the parking lot outside a laundromat, I waited to hear the precise dates on which I could complete this trial run, but Jessica was cooking, and she was telling me about beer can chicken. It was around the Fourth of July. Extensively, she explained the process of creating a chicken cavity and gently inserting a can of Pabst Blue Ribbon and then she described the way the chicken moistened and the way it was better to use a lighter beer and I wondered why we were talking about beer can chicken when there were serious things to talk about like when we could get me on the road but rather than interjecting I made positive and attentive remarks to give the impression of caring deeply about her beer can chicken. "Mmm," I said, "sounds good." Or, "Yummy." And as I thought more about her telling me this I hypothesized that it could only be a good thing that she was sharing the beer can chicken part of her life with me.

Before the first show Jessica handed me the ALL ACCESS laminate, black and orange, I'd wear for the next three months proudly clipped to my hip.

In cursive the laminate read *Stephen Kellogg and the Sixers* and *The Bear*, the album just released and to be promoted, and in cursive it also read *Vanguard*, the band's record label. There was a cubist-looking design of a bear's face, and on the other side the shows were listed, first the date, then the venue, city, and state. Tonight was Connecticut.

Then Vermont, Massachusetts, Michigan, Wisconsin, Illinois, Minnesota, Wisconsin, Iowa, Kansas, Colorado, Colorado, Nebraska, Texas, Texas, Texas, Alabama, Georgia, Tennessee, North Carolina, North Carolina, Virginia, Maryland, Pennsylvania, Vermont, Massachusetts, Pennsylvania, Pennsylvania, Pennsylvania.

Then a ten-day break.

Then New York, New York, Indiana, Missouri, Arizona, California, California, California, California, Oregon, Washington, Washington, North Dakota, Illinois, Ohio, New York, New York.

There were three shows in three days, four shows in four days, five in five, and five in five again. I saw that at one point during the tour we'd be playing seven shows in seven nights in seven different states. There were shows at bars and ballrooms and the House of

Blues, shows at cafés and colleges and the Cat's Cradle, shows at the Fox Theater, the Iron Horse, the Blind Pig. The tour started at Stage One, in the garage of which I crouched, holding a can of black spray paint, methodically coating a metal grate.

"The grates are for the shirt and CD displays," Jessica explained, also crouching, also holding a can. There was a small impression, circular and red, on the tip of my thumb.

I knew it had ultimately been Stephen's decision to bring me along, but I couldn't escape the feeling that if Jessica hadn't approved of me I wouldn't be here. It was she who responded to the email in the first place. It was she who I talked to on the phone all summer. And it was she who had arranged the trip to Columbus. Before I had ever heard Stephen's voice, and certainly before I had met him, it was Jessica who dealt with me. Jessica had been Stephen's tour manager even before the Sixers were a band. She'd finished her last two years of college by earning credits while on the road with him. She was a friendlier—though, at first, not too friendly—Cerberus. Over time I realized her job conflated roles on opposite ends of the personality spectrum: doggishness toward outsiders, patience with insiders. Sometimes situations demanded a mixture of the two.

She always had a plan. And if a predicament arose out of nothing, her first reaction was never to complain, never to assign guilt, never to mope. Before we had a GPS system for the van, she was the one who, before each drive, printed out the map. She knew where we were supposed to be and when we were supposed to be there. Before every show, while the Sixers readied the stage and then waited to sound check, she spoke with the club's manager about setting up the merchandise: when and exactly where and how much space and if the club was to take a cut of the profit. She worked with the fans who volunteered to work the merchandise table in exchange for free entrance. Some nights there was no one to do it; then she told me to do it. After the stage was prepared, and when the Sixers had taken up their instruments, she was the one who stood by the sound technician in his booth, telling him that perhaps Kit's vocals were too high, Sam's guitar too low, because the Sixers, that tour, could not afford their own sound tech, so whoever worked at the venue was the person who controlled the Sixers' sound. During the show she stood by the booth or she stood by the merchandise or she stood backstage or she stood side stage, and after the show she oversaw any of the Sixers who were to sign autographs any given night, and then she oversaw accounting for all the money made from merchandise, and then she oversaw the breaking down of the station, and then she met with the club owner or manager to settle financially, and then she checked us into the hotel, giving us our room assignments. She was our mom and our staff sergeant.

In addition to all of these roles, she was often the only woman. Sometimes another tour manager was a woman or someone who worked at the club or the lead singer of another band, but for the most part this industry was an industry run by men. I wondered what that meant for Jessica. I wondered if it wore on her. And I wondered how.

After that night we played several more shows in New England before turning west. Jessica's apartment in Northampton was our point of departure. We'd be going to Michigan. Kit looked up from the sofa as Boots and Sam and I came through the front door. He said hello. Jessica was sitting by Jesse, her husband, his arm around her shoulder, his lips, hidden in his beard, whispering into her ear. I stood still in the entrance hallway, said nothing. I walked out first, out of her home, out onto the sidewalk toward the van. Boots and Sam followed, then Jessica, then Kit; we took Stephen from his wife and daughters, turned west, away from home, and drove and drove.

Five hours before the show, I helped unload the trailer. I watched Jessica. I learned the process. She took the suitcases out first and used them to hold open the swinging doors. Then we carried everything—instruments, wardrobe bags, amps, microphones, cases of all makes and sizes—from the trailer to the venue, through the front door, past the bar on the left with MAGIC HAT NOW ON DRAFT and BURST SHOTS and CASH ONLY, past the framed photograph of Buddy Holly, past the framed photograph of Elvis Presley, and past the upside-down paper cones covering the spigots of the liquor bottles. We carried everything under the low and dark ceiling, across the white-and-blue tiled floor and past the framed newspaper clip that read "Nirvana lead singer found dead in Seattle."

I was in Ann Arbor, Michigan. I do not remember the show except for the fact that it was Tuesday night, that the crowd was drunk and that I learned how and where to carry these things. Each venue was different but the template was the same.

The next day I struggled to find a position in the van to sleep. I was prone to motion sickness. In the beginning I was unfamiliar with the van and had not yet discovered that if I burrowed myself completely into a blanket, a porous blanket, most particularly the blanket that Kit's mother had made for him, then I could sleep. I did not yet know that if I listened to *August and Everything After* I would fall asleep sometime during "Perfect Blue Buildings." Resting in the van was not yet, though it would be soon, natural.

We arrived in Milwaukee around midnight and in the morning I rose alone, very early, to roam the town and search for solitude. I could not find anything nearby except a shopping mall in which there were some scattered chairs by a coffee kiosk. I sat down.

The road was a plane of extremes. There was first the constrained democracy of the van: driving thousands of miles with five other people within several feet of you, five people talking on the phone, five people clicking their keyboards, five people watching DVDs of Tom Petty, five people choosing their own music, five people telling jokes, telling stories, confessing, laughing. And then there was the arbitrary mob of the show. My relation to this mob became such an act for me that I started to think of the audience as unreal. Quickly into the tour there was a degree of numbness and even malignance in my interactions with the fans. Conversations felt mechanical and rehearsed, and I felt a sort of unreasonable spite, and it was the same way for the staff of the venues. The method of the show was itself a theater, something rehearsed and practiced and, all too often, utterly feigned. If nothing else, I knew I was feigning interest in others. Because I was tired. That was what I told myself. I needed rest. I would never see them again.

And then there were the mornings like this morning when I sought solitude, mornings of coffee shops in foreign towns. Early on, my search for solitude was so artificially created and misguided as to be anything *but* withdrawing from a public space. I called a friend, I wrote an email, I sent a postcard. It was anything but solitude, anything but rest. Early on I could not stop the motion in my head. I took my fetters with me. Commotion reigned. When I was supposed to be roaming the town and searching for solitude, I realized the time had slipped away and I was already back at the venue.

Time was a loop of beginnings and endings, each day four seasons in itself.

Shank Hall in Milwaukee was a big room with a big stage and an island bar. Jessica approached me as I helped unload the trailer; she said the club was twenty-one-and-up. She said she was not sure what the manager would say about me. I wondered why we should tell him at all; he wouldn't ask. But she walked over to him and I watched their conversation, watched him lean to the side, looking past her at me. He said something, she looked back at me and I knew it was bad.

"Side stage," she said when she had come over. "The entire show."

I was isolated to an area of about fifty square feet. It included a bathroom, a chair, and some steps that led up to the stage. It was dark. I tried to read but a headache ensued. When the show started, it was both dark and very loud.

My back against the wall, I watched the twenty-minute opening set of the short blonde girl with a big voice. I was not particularly fond of her music, and I was not particularly fond of her. In Ann Arbor I had, because I was perceived as the smallest fish in the pond, been forced to help her on and off stage; I don't remember her saying thank you. Her music was romantic soul-pop, her lyrics cliché.

Sometimes someone would walk by on the way to the restroom and say something like, That sucks man, or Dude, I'm sorry, or Can I get you something? It was as if they were paying their respects. Valiantly and nobly I assured them everything was quite all right, that I did not need a thing from them.

Patrick was an employee of Shank Hall. I had made sure, per Stephen's code of road ethics, to shake his hand and look him in the eyes. His hand was flaccid, his eyes lazy and limp and shrunken. His hair was wispy. My first assessment was that he was clearly suspicious. Upon further consideration he was, at best, a rogue. But he grew into a slimy villain when, during the set, he returned to the restroom shortly after he had just been and I had said Hello Patrick, applying Stephen's road ethic, and then he left, and then shortly thereafter he returned a third time, and then a fourth, and suddenly my nose detected the earthy stench of marijuana, which explained his passive eyes and his cowardly handshake and the lifeless glaze that resigned him absolutely to everything in this world vivacious. There was nothing I could do in my allotted space except send Jessica messages explaining that the club, which had deemed me, of all twenty-year-olds, a "liability," that was the word they had used, "liability," because I was in the presence of alcohol, that this selfsame club had their own skulking staff smoking pot in the restroom to which I was bound for the entire night.

The learning was steep.

In one of the following days there was a small financial disaster in which the Sixers lost nine hundred dollars. I was told only vaguely about the scenario but afterward was approached by Stephen who said Jessica needed help, that she did too much and that I was going to start having some new responsibilities, an economic stake in the band. It was two in the afternoon and I had eaten nothing that day and my whole body felt congested and it was raining and the sky was a domineering shade of gray. I wanted to go to the pharmacy for medicine, but I sat by Jessica and learned my new duties.

Before each show I would write down, with a pen on a legal pad, the number of each type of shirt, the number of each album and the number of pairs of drumsticks. At the end of the show I was to do the same and then subtract. If the difference added up to the amount of money we had, then nothing had been lost. It was all supposed to even out. I was shown how to take the shirts out of the boxes, and how to put them back in. The same with the CDs. I was shown where the legal pad was kept, where there might be a pen. And it wasn't that this became solely my duty; it was something I did in addition to Jessica. I was a check to the system.

That was in Wisconsin, in September.

I was a minor character, but I was learning my lines.

Late-night and overnight drives became my specialty, something at which I concentrated all my efforts when I heard Stephen say one morning, because I had fallen asleep while sitting in the passenger's seat, "Sharpless is the most worthless wingman we've ever had." After that I was the best wingman they'd ever had. I bought blueberry Pop-Tarts and I bought Skittles and I bought whole milk and Mountain Dew Voltage. When I had a turn to be the DJ, I played Joss Stone and Rage Against the Machine or an episode of "This American Life." And I never fell asleep again, not once. I was the first to get out of the van and the first to open the trailer doors. When we played at a radio station I was the first to crawl over the equipment to snatch the mandolin, to uncover the banjo, which I called the Deceptively Heavy Banjo. I named Allen the Table and I named Pam the Printer, and I was the one to find out where we were to put the empty cases, which were called "deads," and I was the one to pack the trailer, to lock it, to slap it, to walk around the side of the Bear, to shut the door and say, "All set."

I was the first one out.

I was the last one in.

The Sixers were sponsored by Motel 6.

"Motel 6 is happy," said the CEO of Accor North America in an official statement, "to support the dedicated and creative efforts of young musicians," but the youngest of the Sixers was twenty-seven, the oldest thirty-three, and one had two daughters, and one was divorced, and another was married; they were leaving their younger years and entering middle age.

Whenever we stayed at Motel 6 it was only when we had four to six hours before we needed to hit the road again. Customarily we took two rooms for the six of us, so that two of three nights you were not alone in bed, but on Motel 6 nights we got three rooms, each of us getting our own thin mattress with its stiff sheets and rough throw.

The promotion was called "Rock Yourself to Sleep."

Sometimes the Motel 6 rooms were streaked with rust or littered with the corpses of dead bugs or lined with the hair of previous travelers, but on November 1, in the middle afternoon in Indianapolis, the rooms had been pristinely kept. It was a luxury to have time to clean up before the show. No rust, no stains of bodily fluid, no pubic hairs in the bathroom.

I stepped out of the shower, dried off, put on my underwear and walked into the room. I had laid out my clothes onto the bed, a habit of mine: shoes on the floor, socks on the shoes, pants draped over the edge of the bed, belt on the pants, and shirt on the bed. It looked like a person had been sitting comfortably and then had vanished out of their clothes.

"Does this look all right?" I asked Jessica as I pointed to the clothes on the bed. It was a gray v-neck with jeans and a cardigan. I had worn it before.

"Yeah," she said. "Why?"

"My friend is coming tonight."

"Oh, that's right."

"She always dresses well," I said quickly, "so I have to look OK. Does this look OK?"

"It looks great, Sharpless."

The club was another twenty-one-and-up. Nicole and I would not be allowed inside without trickery or negotiation. We could not simply, I thought, waltz through the front door, so I tried to scheme a way inside. As we walked from the Mexican cantina at which we had eaten with Boots and Jon McLaughlin to the club across the street, Jon offered to walk us through the front door. He said they knew him and it would be easy. But I told him I could get us in. I felt that I had earned the right to move some parts and that some of Jessica's authority had trickled down to me, and if not her authority then at least some of her straight-shooter tactics and cleverness. I told Nicole there was a way in the back, but when we walked through the alley behind the club, the gate had been shut and locked.

"Shit," I said.

I approached the gate, on top of which there was barbed wire, and shook it, hearing the high-pitched rattle of the chain links. The fence was only six feet high but the barbed wire was impressive. I put my hands on my hips.

Nicole said, "Here," handing me her purse and looking at me with her honey-brown eyes. I stepped back. She placed one foot in the fence, gripped the metal wiring with her hands, and easily lifted her dancer's body.

"No no no," I said. "Nicole, that's barbed wire," I said watching her scale the fence, holding her purse. "Could you please get down?"

She landed softly.

"Well," I said, "at least you got to meet Jon and Boots." I had given up.

"Hunter," she said, "we'll just walk through the front door."

I wondered if they'd call security, I wondered if they'd call the police, I wondered if the Sixers would get into trouble, if Jessica would, and I wondered if I'd be left alone, if I'd fail the girl, if I'd fail at getting her to the other side of the show.

But we simply waltzed through the front door, untouched and unquestioned.

The lights were low. Women wore dresses, men wore blazers, and everyone held cocktails, beers, or glasses of wine. Hurrying to the dressing room, the bar to our right, the small stage to our left, we followed a hallway to a staircase, the staircase to a basement.

Stephen, Kit, Jon, Sam and Boots sat reviewing lyrics, talking, typing on their phones, changing the strings to guitars, or eating pretzels. Nicole met each of them and I watched proudly the way a young man does when he has the privilege of being with a very beautiful girl at a party where he can impress the important with a girl beyond his own reasonable reach. We went upstairs, because the basement was small.

I stood by her and we watched the set.

Stephen invited Jon to the stage as a song ended. Jon hopped up to the hollers of the hometown crowd and he sat at the piano, brushing his brown hair from his eyes. "Hey hey hey," he said into the microphone. "Check check check. Can you hear me?" Cheers. He dropped his fingers onto the keys, beginning the song.

Under his plaid shirt his shoulders and arms rose and fell, moved. His eyes shut, remained shut, and then opened. The sound of Sam's pedal steel slid underneath the piano, expanding the notes, whining proudly, the volume fluctuating, then the song driving forward as Stephen strummed the rhythm on his guitar, as Boots brushed the crash cymbal, the snare drum, building the beat as Jon began to sing

> She has the power
> With every move she makes
> To turn my eyes
> And turn my fate

Kit moved with the music, head down, left and right, fingering the fat strings of the bass guitar, the tie hanging from his shirt swinging side to side; Sam, at the pedal steel, and Jon, on the piano, paralleled each other, both curling their shoulders, and you could see both their faces absorb their streaking hands across the pedal steel or stabbing, reaching to keys, the lines on their foreheads and cheeks and near their eyes coming together, bunching together, the only difference Jon's moving lips

> I'm gonna throw my love around

Stephen, his beard thick, with a tie and button-down shirt, the sleeves rolled up, approached the microphone, sang the second verse

> In an unfriendly world
> Who cares who you are

On his head was a top hat he had worn the night before in Rochester, New York, where the Sixers had covered a Tom Petty album for Halloween. Stephen nodded back to Jon from the second verse back to the chorus, to the song's final repetitions

> I'll be what I have to be
> And as long as I am
> I'm gonna throw my love around

The song climaxed with Stephen cutting at his guitar, bending with the rhythm, his beard gleaming with sweat, his shirt darkening, climaxed with Jon agonizing at the piano, his eyes narrow, his shoulders, arms, and face contorted, climaxed with Sam scraping the pedal steel, with Kit thumping the bass, with Boots striking the crash.

From Indiana we drove south into Texas. Normally Texas was so expansive you looked out the window and saw endless horizon. Texas was everything. There were swamps and there were deserts. There were mountains and plains. There were meadows and forests. There was not one thing Texas was not. But we could see none of it now, because it was completely dark.

Because we were in Texas, because this was my home, I couldn't sleep. I simply sat on the first bench of the van and looked out the window. There was nothing. Only billboards, exit signs, other cars. All of these I paid great and lonely attention to. I didn't know what I expected. I looked at the writing on these signs for signs of things I knew, signs of the familiar, restaurants at which I had eaten before, cities to which I had been before, as if the signs possessed jetsam of my scattered self.

Stephen and Jessica were driving.

I was reverently quiet and felt the good-sad feeling of nostalgia but they were not quiet. They started trading comments back and forth. Jokes, jokes about cowboys and racists and religious fundamentalists. These were the sorts of things we as Texans heard all the time. I pretended to laugh as they joked but I never felt further away from them than I did as we drove darkly into Texas. Stephen wasn't my inspirer, Jessica not my sister, this not my van nor this my tour or band or music or life. They kept talking. I'd pretended to laugh but soon I grew tired of the jokes. Soon I grew passive and expressionless. I hated them. This was my home. But I said nothing.

"Texas has actually been really good to us," Stephen said. But it was too late and he knew it was too late. Jessica looked at me in the rearview mirror.

I stood in the hotel parking lot, looking at the cityscape I knew.

The abstract ways in which people responded to hearing that I was on the road with a rock band were, compared to the concrete numbers of the roads on which we drove, the names of the rivers we crossed and the restaurants in which we ate, obscene. They said I was lucky, they said I was living the dream, and they asked if the road was different and what it was like; it was not unlike anything else. The words "lucky" and "dream" were thrown around. They cast a pall over what mattered to me. I had heard these words, sometimes feigning participation in a conversation outside a venue with a fan, and I had read these words, on awestruck faces as if I lived the life of a god, in a world with no hospitals or skinned knees, but in the end my dreams were plagued with the ache for rest, and the only luck was the luck of a better cup of coffee. To hear those words and see the look on someone's stupid face was to feel and be isolated, unable to express the reality of the road. There was nothing golden about anything. It was nothing and nothing; nothing was golden. Some nights the music approached what seemed to be something spiritual, something glorious and sacred and hallow that was not an escape but an enhancement, an inflection to a life already lived, but for every song that Stephen sang ascending steps to heaven, there were restless nights in motels, drunk fans, endless stretches of gray interstate, and the absolute inability of anyone besides those in the van to know anything about the road. Because of this the five others became the only people I knew. When friends or family members visited me at shows, it made me sick to speak about the road. What they wanted to talk about or what they expected was not what I had to offer. This happened over and over until I started to wonder, then, if the fault lay not with the person who wanted to hear about my travels but in my own ability to express. I wondered if I was just choosing the wrong details or subscribing to the wrong pattern already laid out.

What I knew I would remember—because I learned gradually to anticipate the things I would remember, though of course I was always surprised—was the Chinese food in Austin the next day that I ordered for Jessica and me, and I remember the host saying it would be ready in fifteen minutes and I remember sweating in the Texas sun but thinking that to sweat in Austin is only right and I remember the barista in the coffee shop wearing a new-leaf green shirt and I remember his rat-tail and his frail frame. We were disappointed, Jessica and I, by the Chinese food. We set up the merch. We waited for the show. When the show started we were bothered by the Austin crowd which, because it was Austin, believed it knew what live music should be. We watched as Stephen dismissed the others from the stage. We watched as he played, alone with his guitar, "Satisfied Man," and we watched as the crowd gave itself to the song, to silence. We ate breakfast the next morning at La Reyna on South 1st Street. Our waitress was old and wrinkled and plump, and the wonderful brown skin above her eyes was painted turquoise, beautifully and intensely turquoise spilling into the dark and crinkly brown folds of her fleshy eyelids. One of us remarked that chips and salsa was odd with coffee, one of us asked for chocolate-chip waffles which they did not have, and one of us ordered lunch instead of breakfast.

We drove north on Interstate 35 out of Austin, drove north past Georgetown and past Temple and past Moody and past Waco and past Hillsborough and past Waxahachie. We got off the interstate and onto Royal Lane. We got off Royal Lane and onto Snow White Drive. We ate at my home. I remember my mom opening the front door and walking happily, smiling, down our sidewalk under the oak and to the van, but I don't remember anything we said inside.

In middle autumn, before a two-week break in the tour, Kit and Jessica and I spent time in Northampton, Massachusetts, at Jessica's home. We had just played in Maryland and now had a short break before several more shows, and then it would be the halfway point of the tour.

Besides Vermont, Massachusetts has the best American autumn. I felt this was not a matter of opinion but a scientific fact. Crescent Drive, the street on which Jessica lived, turned and curved out of sight as I took a walk into town, the leaves on the trees above red and yellow and fiery orange, pods of the sun, captors of its light against the gray of the road. The trees made a thick and colorful canopy. Leaves had fallen onto the roofs of houses, onto parked cars, onto the porches of houses and into the baskets of bicycles, onto grills and onto coolers, in between cracks of wood and onto trash bins, as if the whole earth were flocked with the ripest colors heaven could grow.

The town itself was blue jeans and Boston Red Sox caps. There were tattoos and dreadlocks and hooligan teenagers. There were homeless people and businessmen and women and people on buses and people on bikes and people running and people jogging and people walking, people in their town; they worked. It was morning and this was their town and they loved their town. It was autumn, a beautiful autumn day, and every movement glowed with the purpose of morning and of work. They played their part. They attended school. They lived their day.

That night, in Jessica's home, the air inside warm against the chill of fall, the couch worn, the television showing a football game, the decorations on the wall specific and holy and personal to the inhabitants of the house rather than the hotel art to which I had grown accustomed, this along with the sounds from the kitchen, the metallic clanging of pans, the hum of the refrigerator door when it was opened, and Jessica's sporadic footsteps; this was home.

She loved to cook. I considered my courting the Sixers the summer before to have been successful in large part because I listened to Jessica's explanation of beer can chicken. She loved good food. Sam and I were the most heinous offenders on the road because of our predilection to cheeseburgers and nachos and buffalo sauce. I remember a distinct moment in which, on a sunny morning in Montana, after dispersing from the van to search for food, Sam went one way, and Jessica went the other. I stood by the van. I had not yet chosen.

Jessica brought in a tray of crackers, cheese and Honeycrisp apples, about which she was particularly excited, apples with a cool crunch. Kit provided a red wine from Spain and we ate.

In her home, we were royalty.

"Cousin," we said. "This is delicious."

At first I had been apprehensive about calling her Cousin, because she was not my cousin but Stephen's cousin. At first I called her Jessica. Then I called her Jess. And then after hearing Sam and Boots and Kit call her Cousin, I called her Cousin. She reminded me of my mom, felt like a sister, but I called her Cousin, because that was her name and that, I thought, was what you called people when you felt very close to them, as close as family, but were not actually related.

We sat at the kitchen table and she brought out chicken Parmesan and a salad of fresh lettuce, goat cheese, and the Honeycrisp apples.

We drank wine until we began to impersonate Stephen and something he had said during a show. He had been drinking moderately and had said to the crowd, mostly as a joke for us, "This might be the alcohol talking, but I think I like you guys."

We started the impersonations modestly.

"This might be the alcohol talking," Jessica said, "but this is the best fucking salad I've ever had."

We grew bolder.

"This might be the alcohol talking," Kit said, "but I do believe Sharpless is learning how to woo women because of *my* expertise."

And then I grew confessional and dramatic.

"This might be the alcohol talking," I said, raising my glass of wine as if making a toast, securing the gazes of Kit and Cousin, hearing myself say winefully, "but I've got a pretty small penis."

During the ten-day break in the middle of the tour Jessica dyed a strand of her hair purple; she also sliced her right hand open while carving a pumpkin. As I unwrapped the bandage I thought about all the times I had seen Jessica take a stern voice with someone, the times I had seen her strong in a tense situation, the times I had seen her have grace under pressure, but now, as I got closer to the gash, the lights of the hotel bathroom bright and fluorescent, she whimpered. The light showed the cut was not wide but very deep and swollen. Ten stitches held the two ridges of bright pink skin together. Jessica was making a face in the mirror as I cleaned the cut with an iodine swab. Stephen's head appeared in the doorway. He asked her something and while they spoke I tried to work very quickly, cleaning the cut, then bringing the torn edges of skin together and fastening them with a Band-Aid. She asked how it looked. I lied and said it was healing admirably, not mentioning the creamy white pus that had oozed out.

"Thank you, Nurse Hunter," she said when I was done.

For the first few days after the wound, Jessica tried to act as if nothing had happened. She would pick up the merchandise grates or a box of t-shirts or she would attempt to help with one of the amps, but then found she couldn't. She needed an extra hand. When she drove she grasped the steering wheel with her left hand and rested her right very lightly on the opposite end. Her lame hand couldn't grab or twist or pry, so when she wanted a sip of coffee, or when she wanted a bottle opened, or when she wanted a piece of Laffy Taffy or a Jolly Rancher to keep her awake, I handed her the cup, unscrewed the bottle cap, or placed the piece of candy in a very specific nook of her injured hand, which seemed to always be in a half-open, half-closed position.

We sat now in the van driving from San Francisco to Anaheim. We had just stopped at IHOP and after eating my chocolate-chip pancakes I opened the Styrofoam box and looked at her sandwich.

"It's cut into fourths," I said.

"Oh," she said, "you mean like a club sandwich?"

This was when I learned that club sandwiches were cut into fourths.

"Do you want it now?" I asked.

"Touch the sandwich," she said.

I did.

"Is it soggy?"

"No."

"Great, give me some fries."

I commenced to hand her French fries one by one, and then the sandwich, occasionally rearranging the lettuce or chicken or bacon, evenly distributing the ingredients so that each bite could be in top form, containing all the tastes. I learned the order and manner in which she ate her meals. As I fed her I told her about a girl I had fallen in love with the day before.

I had first seen her while I was cleaning out the van. She wore blue jeans and a cream top, her hair was blonde and wavy, and her body was of divine proportions. And on her lovely hip was clipped an ALL ACCESS laminate.

Who's that? I had wondered to myself.

When I had made my way inside the venue later, setting my things down and plugging in the printer, there she was. We were alone together in the dressing room.

"Hi," she said. Her voice was perky.

"Hello," I said, and then, filled with courage, "How are you?"

"Good," she said, and introduced herself.

I thought about her. She was the girlfriend of the other band's drummer. But maybe she wasn't into him because she had sounded perky when we spoke. Because of me? Maybe. She was perky, yes. Maybe she wasn't into him. Maybe she wasn't into her boyfriend and was looking for someone a little younger maybe or maybe some kind of fling or maybe an alcohol-induced affair.

"She has such pretty shoulders," I told Jessica. "She's so fucking hot."

There was interstate ahead.

"You think so? I think she's just OK."

"No way," I said. "There's something about her. I would lick mayonnaise off her body if she spilled it on herself, and I hate mayonnaise."

"What?"

"I said I would lick mayonnaise off her body if she spilled it."

And then I attempted charades, playing the part of the girl-friend at first, with mayonnaise on my chest, and then I played my own part, licking the mayonnaise off her erect nipple.

"That's messed up, Sharpless."

On a different drive in California, late at night after a show, trying to fall asleep on the first bench, I heard Jessica say, "I've got to climb back, so watch out," and as she clambered over me her foot stepped dangerously near my penis.

"Whoa," I said. "Watch out! You almost stepped on Tic-Tac."

She stopped.

"Wait, who is Tic-Tac?" she asked.

"Oh, no," I said. I knew I had divulged too much. I felt the steady friction of the van speeding along the empty interstate in the time between the late night and early morning when I should have been asleep and because of that I felt the exhaustion and unreality of having been woken in the middle of the night with the blanket still cocooned around me and still in a sort of dream state and so I said, "Tic-Tac is"—and I heard Stephen getting up on the bench behind me and saw Jessica still standing over me and felt Kit, driving, looking at me through the mirror—"my penis."

"What!"

She started to laugh.

"Sharpless," Stephen said from another bench, "who gave it that nickname?"

He sounded concerned like a father; he sat up and his face showed concern too.

"I did," I confessed.

In the front of the van Kit was laughing, saying over and over, "Holy shit, holy shit."

"Hunter," Jessica said, also sounding a bit concerned now, her laughter having subsided, "why would you call your own penis Tic-Tac?"

It was the truth, and it was such a success that Kit, as soon as he had access to the Internet, incorporated it into my email address with the band. The name later stuck, and came emblazoned on the official Stephen Kellogg and the Sixers team jacket the band gave me as a gift.

The night I snapped was cold and dark. In the morning it had been snowing light and soft flakes, but in the evening the temperature rose just above freezing, it rained, and my breath turned to smoke. I had done laundry. I wore a red stocking cap that said *Amsterdam*; Jessica had given it to me in Northampton. We were in Spokane, Washington. Tomorrow we'd start the journey east, home. I was sitting in the dressing room after the set. I was trying to write about the set. The Sixers had started with "Born in the Spring" which I thought was a good song to open with but when they had started to play the song Stephen's microphone cut out after about thirty seconds. They had to repeat the process and the rest of the show was affected. I was writing these things down and other things about how one thing like that, one unexpected turn changes the mind not only of the performer but of the viewer, the one participating in the act as a member of the audience, when my phone vibrated. It was a text message from Jessica. I was tired. She needed me to retrieve something from the van: two vouchers for the free rooms at Motel 6. I pulled them out of a bin and saw that each sheet was composed of three vouchers. I brought them to Jessica.

I lied quickly, "I didn't know if you wanted me to get two sheets or two vouchers."

I don't know why I lied.

"That's six," she said. She gave a short laugh without smiling, keeping her eyes on me the whole time. "We only needed two." She tore two off and handed me the rest. "Put those back in the van."

"No," I said. I looked at her. "I'm not going to make another fucking trip to the van just to put those back. It's freezing."

Sam and Kit stood nearby and I was aware of them watching.

"I just don't want them to get separated from the rest," she said.

"Well you're fucking welcome," I said, and as she opened her mouth and started to protest I walked away, turning my back.

I saw her at other points in the night—in the elevator, at the merch table, loading out—but we said nothing. On the drive home I remembered that not only were we sharing a room that night, but we were sharing a bed.

Sam watched TV.

Jessica stood in the bathroom. The door was cracked.

I got up and walked over to her.

"Hi," I said. I felt like a child.

She opened the door.

"I wanted to say sorry," I said. "I let circumstances get the best of me."

"It's OK. This one gets a hug."

In the end words are poor things. They are gestures. I doubted my ability to express to others what the road was like. It was the road. The words I spoke, the lines I wrote were flimsy imitations of what had actually happened, wayward fingers attempting to apprehend experience. Experience I experienced with others. I tried but I felt, mostly, that I failed. Words are of course suggestions. I began to question the process of representation. Like photographs of a Cézanne there were no actual strokes, was no texture, no depth. You can only make out the vague colors. The photograph suggests the texture, and that is where you place your hope. If there is any texture at all, any depth or reality, it is translated.

4

Steamer

IN SICILY THE SUN was setting, Mount Etna in the distance a mass of fading whites and blues dissolving into sky. Stephen walked with Sam, who was not yet a member of the band. Having just left the restaurant they were full of food and warm with wine. They were making their way back to the hotel for a night's rest before, the next morning, playing a show for the American military base at Sigonella. While they walked together either Stephen said to Sam, "Man, I think you should be in this band," or Sam said to Stephen, "Man, I think I should be in this band." But despite their inability to remember who brought up the idea, it is certain the listener responded by saying, "Yeah, I think so too."

Sam was, at that time in his life, the lead guitarist for the touring band of Kate Voegele, an actress and musician. Because of her popularity, Kate did not have to tour all year long. And when she was on the road, she toured on a bus, which meant the ability to both play—on a tour bus, the driver is sealed off from the cabin, allowing the consumption of alcohol—and rest—tour buses are equipped with a space for six to eight bunk beds, curtained off from the noise.

In contrast, the Sixers were sometimes on the road nine or ten months out of the year. And for those nine or ten months out of the year, they toured in the Bear. Dusty, cramped, curtainless.

Sam was from Ohio. The Sixers were from New England.

Sam had not gone to college. The Sixers met in college.

Sam had been making good, reliable money with Kate. His position in her band was dependable and also carried with it—because Kate was young, pretty, and played mainstream pop—the lurking potential for a hit single to launch her career from relatively popular to limitlessly known.

The Sixers were neither topping charts nor consistently selling out venues. Even when they met Sam they were a road-weary trio whose careers, at least in terms of sales, had spiked early and steadily dwindled since. *Bulletproof Heart*, the Sixers' first studio album, had sold around ten thousand copies. Universal Records then considered them worth a shot, signing them in 2005—a signing the band celebrated by skydiving—and releasing their self-titled *Stephen Kellogg and the Sixers*. The album sold around thirty thousand copies, but it wasn't enough for Universal, who dropped the Sixers. They landed with a smaller label, but each album—*Glassjaw Boxer*, twenty-two thousand units sold, and now *The Bear*, seventeen thousand sold—generated less and less profit.

It was in the midst of this trajectory that the Sixers, on a cruise ship called the Rock Boat, a floating music festival that sailed from Miami to ports in Jamaica and the Grand Cayman Islands, met Sam.

Boots was watching the stage. A composite band made of an ever-changing combination of musicians from the nearly thirty groups aboard the ship played an endless improvisation. On the corner of the stage there was a shaggy-haired man bent over a pedal steel. It was Sam. Boots left the stage and found Stephen. "You've got to see this guy," he said. The drummer and frontman then went to the stage and watched Sam, sitting on a small stool, a beer at his feet, his hands sliding across the long metallic strings of the steel. When the musicians dispersed Stephen took Sam aside. They went to the cafeteria and ate ice cream. They talked about the boat, about life as a musician, about life as a married musician, and about the future.

The boat returned to shore, Sam to Ohio, the Sixers to New England, and more than a year later the Sixers invited Sam, who had time off from Kate's band, to join them for four weeks in Europe, and it was on that trip, in Sicily, that the decision was made to make Sam a Sixer. Stephen told him, "You'll be making half the money doing twice the work," and he joined.

I met Sam in the Philadelphia airport. With a Styrofoam box stuffed with Chinese food I sat by him at our gate, from which we'd fly to New York City to join the others. Sam wore sneakers, gray pants, a cardigan and a shirt with the words FT. LAUDERDALE SPRING BREAK. Steamer was his nickname, but he was sometimes known as, because of his proclivity to small talk and fine drink, Social Steamer. He had a nose ring. His hair was dirty blonde, as was the dusting of stubble across his face. He told me he loved Ohio, Cleveland especially, and that when he was not on the road he worked at American Greetings recording tracks for e-cards. While scrolling the touchscreen of his phone he told me of his father, a federal prosecutor, his mother, who had homeschooled Steamer and his siblings, and his wife, a teacher, whose name was tattooed across his left forearm—Stefanie—so that when he reached his hand high up the neck of his guitar during a show, she was with him.

He met his wife at a summer camp after seventh grade. Sam and a group of his friends commandeered a van together, but before the trip started he was told to go to another van. He was not happy. But when he opened the door there, sitting on the first bench, was Stef: high-cheeked and sharp-nosed with measured eyes. ("It was kind of majestic," he would later recall.) She was from one end of Ohio, and he was from the other. After camp they wrote letters and, on Sunday nights, when it was cheaper to make long-distance calls, they spoke on the phone. Sam's mom kept a running tab on the Sunday-night phone bill, and he paid it off penny by penny. Sam and I had both grown up in conservative Christian homes. He was the youngest in the band, new as a member, and I was the youngest in the van, new to the road.

I was a virgin.

The Egg, a spaceship-shaped theater in Albany, New York, had a security guard with a list and a very serious face. At first, waiting to grant us entrance to the underground parking lot, he seemed to doubt our credentials and identifications. When we got through we unloaded from the lot up a crate elevator to the back of the stage; it was all very secretive. Upstairs there was a buffet, one of the best on the road, with an entire basket of dinner rolls of which I ate many. I sat down alone, the first to eat the feast, and then Kit and Sam joined me.

On either side of me they instructively and very seriously explained and recommended some techniques I ought to use in my first experience, whenever that would be, of sexual intercourse.

"Let *her* go down on you first," Kit said, "and finish you down there."

I chuckled, they did not.

This was not, evidently, a chuckling matter.

"That way, you won't come so fast when you start doing it."

"Yeah, yeah," Sam agreed. "And do that *especially* on your first time, because," and he looked mischievously at Kit, at me, "you don't want to last two minutes!"

Kit nodded. "Right, Sam. Then, Hunter, when she's done down there, *you* go down on *her*."

"Okay."

"And when you go down on her," Sam said, "that gets *you* excited after you've already jizzed."

"Exactly."

"Aw," Sam said, patting my back. "Little Hunter."

Stephen sang the songs, Boots cracked the jokes, and Goose did the dance.

They each had a set of routines, talents and characteristics for which they were known among their fans. They had been together for years and had spent nights and days inventing, then developing and finally perfecting these roles. In the beginning Sam had no role. When the sound turned off that night in Iowa, and when Stephen led the Sixers to the precipice of the stage to sing, acoustically, "Milwaukee," the original trio was bright under the lights above, and Sam was unnoticeable, swallowed immutably in the darkness a step behind the others.

Sam's displacement was not an effect of Stephen Kellogg and the Sixers being complete as a trio. They tried their best on any given stage before Sam joined: Stephen front and center, Boots stage right on the drums, and Kit stage left. When the trio played together, however, it was not only the music that sounded disjoint-ed—one guitar was not enough—but even the spatial arrange-ment, the distribution of bodies on the stage looked unnatural. When Sam joined, the stage felt full, the music thick, but at first the balance still seemed contrived.

At the Blind Pig in Ann Arbor the stage was compact, tight with amps and instruments and the bodies of the Sixers as they took their places: Boots on the drums, Stephen at the microphone, Kit on the keys.

Sam stood somewhere in the space between the drums and keys. He was pushed back several feet from the front of the stage.

The show started.

Stephen, Kit and Boots moved with the beat of "Sweet So-phia," moved their hips, their heads, their hands, Stephen and Kit lifting their guitars in the air at the same time, backing off the mi-crophones at the same time.

Sam swayed but did not move, his feet sewn into the floor, his body not defined in itself but seen only in relation to the bod-ies around him, the bodies of Stephen, Kit and Boots, all three of whom were anchored—as Sam was not—to microphones.

Sam's affection for food and drink was unparalleled among the Six-ers. No one contemplated the small things as he did.

After the cake mishap in Northampton—the night I had en-tered the show at the wrong time—Boots, Sam and I stayed at a Motel 6. I sat on the first bench of the van with the cake in a big white box in my lap. Boots drove. Sam navigated. I opened the lid. The cake was very tall and very moist, layered with creamy white icing. I could smell the coffee flavoring. It was not the sort of cake one even attempted to eat with one's hands. We had realized this at the venue and now stopped at a pizza parlor on the edge of town. As I opened the door I saw the only person inside was the man behind the counter. I had volunteered to procure some plastic forks because, I thought, if I succeeded in what might be a precarious situation I would earn accolades from the others. The man behind the counter was clean-shaven. His skin and dark pomaded hair gave him the look of a Neapolitan. His ears were pierced.

"Uh," I said. I hesitated and then asked if I might be able to have three plastic forks.

"You gonna buy anything?"

I said no but assured him that my friend would soon be patronizing his fine establishment. (Indeed, Stephen had told us at the venue he'd be grabbing a slice at this pizzeria, justifying our utensil looting. Later we would discover he went straight to his hotel.)

He looked at me. He was very Italian-looking. This was Massachusetts and this was his pizzeria. He handed me the forks and I left.

On the way to Motel 6, Sam burst out in song, joyous song, a spontaneous improvisation praising in verse and chorus the cake's moisture, icing, even existence, a beautiful song with pauses here and there to find the words to string together a fluid tune. By the third chorus Boots was singing harmonies. In our rooms we ate the cake out of the box and watched *Made* on MTV.

Sam used his phone to find restaurants, but the places he took us to were almost always places he had been before; he was like a truck driver who returned faithfully to the same interstate diner. One night after arriving late in Milwaukee we sat in the van in the parking lot of a hotel. Sam took his phone, scrolled for a minute, his face lighted by the screen, and then with a look of profound relief said, "Oh! They have Rock Bottom!" He lit up and looked at our dark, tired faces as though this were greatly unexpected news. Rock Bottom Brewery, however, could be found by the Atlantic

Ocean and by the Pacific Ocean, could be found in more than fifteen states.

Pumpkin ale in particular perked Sam's mood, and since we were on the road in the fall it was frequently available. In California we were opening shows for Tyrone Wells, who invited us to spend a night at his home in Chino, a town outside of Los Angeles. We arrived at three in the morning and when I woke I smelled the pungent smell of cow shit. Chino, apparently, boasted a thriving cattle industry. Dragging our suitcases and duffle bags to the front door we were greeted by Elina, Tyrone's Hawaiian-born wife. She was short with dark hair and her eyes were like turned-over crescent moons. Tyrone, now embracing her, was nearly six and a half feet tall, pale and bald. For a son they had a small black dog named Pono, who was an icon among Tyrone's devoted fans. Elina led us inside and showed us where we could sleep. She had prepared six beds, each with a towel and washcloth. On the counter in the kitchen there was cheese and wine and while most of us took a glass of water before we went to bed, when Sam saw the refrigerator door open, and when Sam heard Tyrone say, "We have a variety of beers as well," and as soon as Sam heard Tyrone say, in his listing of those varieties, "pumpkin ale," Sam's body straightened and he said, "Oh! I might have one of those!" I myself found a bag of homemade cookies, of which Sam also took part.

The longer I was on the road the more I understood Sam's need to visit places he'd already been. It had something to do with the constant motion and every time you went to a town you'd been to before it didn't mean it was the same. Maybe some buildings had been knocked down, or renovated. Restaurants closed, were bought out. Conglomerate chains of restaurants or coffee shops were attractive because what I wanted was exactly what I was going to get and there was a sort of comfort in a specific expectation meeting the small reality, even if the reality was a cup of coffee or a hamburger. There was comfort when memory and—at the exact instant-now of the coffee being slid across the dark counter and the known logo and known smell and known mass-produced decorations on the wall and the familiar uniforms of the employees—the thing memory suggested turned out to be the same thing. It was comforting and gave me strength but I wondered if it also was a trap. I remember when I was in Colorado trying to find a place to write. I had gotten up as usual before the others and the air was thin and crisp, quick and cold and a light breeze blew and I walked from the hotel into a shopping plaza, a comforting strip mall, and after one cup of coffee looked for another and it was only after I had sat down and looked through the window that I saw the Rocky Mountains.

Sam noticed small things and I liked to think that I, in some small way, noticed small things too. There was a restaurant called Roots on the Square. It was clean and neat, the walls dark and covered with art that was not produced in a factory. The waitresses were tattooed. Our table was thick and wooden, with no wobble whatsoever. We celebrated the table and since Skunk told us the meal was on him, we all ordered fruit smoothies and coffee, except for Sam who did not drink coffee. Our waitress was quite tall and had green eyes.

"She's pretty," Sam said looking after her.

I agreed. I noted her admirable skin.

"Yeah," Sam said. "She really has nice skin."

"She has a nose ring," I said. "I like nose rings."

"Huh, I didn't see it."

"It was on this side." I touched the right side of my nose.

"Opposite of mine." He touched the left side of his nose.

Sometimes he drank too much. I learned this but I also learned it had been worse with Kate. It was not so bad now. When he played with Kate his skill had been such that he did not really need his mind to play the songs. The Sixers were past their days of constant revelry. Their bodies were not the same as they had been. Sam was drunk one night in Minneapolis, at the Fine Line Music Cafe, and when I went to the stage one last time to check for anything we had possibly left, Sam was standing idly there, his weight shifting as though he were underwater, his eyes red, his mouth turning up into a happy smile when he saw me. "Hey man," he said, and slowly walked toward me. The venue was empty. He then rested both hands on my shoulders, using me as support. He looked me in the eye, his breath warm and smelling of beer, and said, "I love you."

We were in the van in the empty parking lot of a twenty-four-hour restaurant in the northeast corner of Iowa at midnight.

"What was that look?" Sam asked Stephen. "You looked at me during the set."

"It was only a look," Stephen said. "You're just perceiving that it was something else."

We—Kit, Jessica, Boots, me—waited. We were tired. We sat and we waited for Sam and Stephen.

"It seemed like you were telling me I was doing something wrong," Sam said.

"It was only a look."

Sam noticed every detail before, during and after a show. Whenever we unloaded the stage and started to pull the amps, instruments and stands from their cases, Sam waved his arms and showed us precisely where each thing went. He had already spoken to the club's employees so he even knew where the dead cases went. He had examined every square inch of cable and space to most efficiently create the stage. Each stage was vastly different from the one before it. A different shape, a different size, a different way to get onto it. Sam took over stage creation. He was even particular about the way we carried certain instruments, about the way we unpacked them, and about the order in which we unpacked them. "No, no," he'd say as I pulled out the banjo. "Let's get acoustic number two." During the show he noticed and noted the body movement and eyes of each band member, the angle at which they raised their guitar. His mind was a pen and spiral notebook. After each show he replayed the details, and after each show he carefully wiped down the strings of his pedal steel. Each instrument had a correct way to be packed and an incorrect way to be packed.

"The look" ended as something of a stalemate and we got out of the van. Stephen ordered a Caesar salad. Sam and I bought chocolate-chocolate-chip muffins.

Great Day St. Louis, a segment on KMOV, was featuring two authors, a seamstress, a band—us—and a chef who showed the camera how to more effectively store spices. These were the sorts of morning shows on which the Sixers played across the country. Once there was a woman with a book on love and food; Stephen and Sam, both of whom stayed alert for ways to romance their wives, were particularly interested. The woman's primary insight was to make love before, rather than after, dinner. In Virginia there was a woman advising the audience about buying international plane tickets, and another who educated children with special needs. At a television studio in Colorado the space was entirely absent of crew, as the cameras were controlled remotely, behind closed doors; it gave the feeling of a sci-fi movie. In Portland a man had made a documentary on air drumming, having just returned from Finland, the home of the World Championships of air guitar.

Hulk Hogan was the first guest, touring a memoir. Then there was the seamstress, sewing scarves, dyeing them, and then there was the chef with the excess spices.

The premier guest, though, on the morning of November 2 on Great Day St. Louis, was a man who had written a book called *The No-Gossip Zone*, or a man who had, in actuality, co-written, with a woman named Bridget Sharkey, a book called *The No-Gossip Zone*. He was the husband of Dr. Laura Berman, a sex therapist who made regular appearances on the Oprah Winfrey Show. His hair was thin, and his facial hair was trimmed to suspicious perfection.

He had been interviewed by FOX NEWS in Chicago, FOX NEWS in Boston, FOX NEWS in New York, FOX NEWS in Detroit, and NEWS CHANNEL 8. We, however, standing idly in the studio, were watching his interview on channel 4, LIVE and RIGHT NOW.

On the program that morning there was a collage clip of people being interviewed about gossip. A man in a t-shirt said we as human beings gossip everywhere. A woman with shiny earrings and a shiny necklace and a shiny purse said, "I work for a major airline," and talked about high gossip. A balding man said, "It's just our social nature."

After a commercial break the host and the author resumed the interview on some couches, and the host said, "The author of *The No-Gossip Zone* says people think of gossip as a lubricant," and the author of *The No-Gossip Zone* said, "I'm the boss of the office."

He said, "It's good to be the boss."

He quoted the Bible—"Number nine: Thou shall not bear false witness against thy neighbor"—he quoted a proverb from the seventeenth century—"A fish rots from the head down"—and he talked economics—"Unprofitable"—"Unprofitable behavior"— "No unprofitable behavior is allowed."

He said all these things as if all things could be quantified.

After KMOV we ate lunch, and Sam introduced me to something to which I would be addicted from then on: buffalo sauce.

And the various types!

Sometimes thicker, even a little chunky—what are the chunks?—and sometimes spicy and hot so that you ate your meal very quickly and quietly with intermittent sips of water and finishing before everyone else to sit and listen and sip your water more as the hotness subsided. Sometimes a thinner, brighter orange; this was the not-so-high-quality stuff. Sometimes, there being a buffalo sauce you judge based on its appearance, on its consistency, its color, even the container it came in, but—after even a bite!—discovering it to be something different, something especially wonderful. So I sat there and ate my buffalo chicken sandwich with Sam. I was very grateful even though this buffalo sauce was the not-so-high-quality stuff, enjoying it all the same. After lunch and after coffee and a donut, we drove to the St. Louis Children's Hospital.

Christy Merrell met us at the circle drive of the hospital. She shook our hands. She said, "The kids are gonna love this!" She moved her face into a smile. She wore a green sweater. She wore glasses. She wore her hair spiked. She helped by carrying a guitar. She led us from the circle drive to the lobby of the hospital, and she led us from the lobby of the hospital to an elevator, which took us to the eighth floor. She led us to a sanitary-smelling playroom. She handed us yellow anti-germ masks. She showed us the stage: several steps wedged into the corner of the room, by a purple crate of books. She showed us the camera, which would broadcast the songs the Sixers played to children as young as five, to whom the song "Ronald MacDonald" might speak, to children as old as seventeen, to whom the song "Wagon Wheel" might speak. She showed us the four rows of child-sized chairs, blue, in front of the stage.

We set our things down by a green box of Legos.

Nurses made pictures with digital cameras.

Nurses introduced me to Michael, who marched directly to the toys. His skin was light brown and he had brown eyes, a curved cleft pallet and a bent nose like a fighter. His teeth were caved in. He wore a white hospital gown patterned with colorful fish. Michael and I commenced to play action figures. He exercised a great affection for them: kicking, punching, slamming, throwing, biting. We moved to trains. He derailed his train, crashed it into a stop sign and I said, "I don't think the train is supposed to do that," and we laughed.

The Sixers then took the stage, or the steps, wearing button-downs and fedoras and the yellow anti-germ masks pushed below their chins. They played "Wheels on the Bus" and "See You Later, See You Soon" and I watched, sitting by Michael in one of the small chairs, and I was thinking I had never seen the Sixers laugh as they were laughing now, had never seen them joke this way or pluck the banjo this way. Had never seen this. Then I saw Stephen's face drop a little, and I looked behind me.

A girl had been wheeled into the room, wheeled by her parents—orbiting the chair like satellites. The girl was tube-laced, bruise-painted. But, Christy told us, it was time to go, time to visit Joe, so we followed Christy past rooms, past nurses, and past doctors to Joe's room.

Joe lay in bed. Tubes like roots, digging into his arms, his throat. The tubes ran to other tubes, attached to medical things, which held sacks of fluid, ran to medical things blinking, clicking, flashing and beeping. Under Joe's eyes hung purple half-moons.

We filed into the room: Christy, Stephen, Jessica, me, Boots, Kit, Sam.

Beep.

Joe's dad was in the room. He said hello, smiled. Joe said hello, winced, and told us his story.

"I got in the pool, swam for a few minutes, and then I got out and I was covered in bruises," he said. His breath was short. "Next day mom took me to the doctor, and then she said that I had leukemia. First day, uh, I was not feeling good, was kind of tired. A few days later, um, I met Christy, and then when I was in this room, in the bone marrow unit, she showed me a video game, *Guitar Hero*! And I started playing her guitar, and then I started, you know, wanting my own."

We were quiet.

"Guess you're a big Beatles fan, huh?" Stephen asked.

There were Beatles posters on the walls.

"Yeah," Joe's dad said, "loves'em."

I watched Christy. She looked happy. Strange to be happy in the room of a dying boy.

Beep, BEEEEEP, beep.

"That's so cool," Stephen said. "We do too."

I watched the tubes, trying not to.

"Well, gang," Stephen said, "there's gotta be something we can play from the Beatles—Sam?"

We all looked at Sam.

BEEEEEP.

Sam said, "Yeah."

He grabbed a guitar.

Nervously strummed it.

He said, "I think we know 'Blackbird.'"

And he said, "We know 'Blackbird,' right?"

The Sixers sang the Beatles,

> Take these broken wings
> And learn to fly
>
> Take these sunken eyes
> And learn to see
>
> Blackbird fly
> Blackbird fly
>
> Blackbird singing in the dead

Joe smiled. His feet shuffled at the foot of the bed, underneath the hospital blanket.

The song finished, we clapped.

Then Joe nodded to his dad, who took something from a table, a pair of John Lennon sunglasses.

"Those are awesome!"

"Joe can play the guitar, too," said Christy.

Christy and Joe looked at each other as if they shared a secret. Joe took the guitar from his father. It looked bulky in his arms as he lay in bed. He put his left hand on the neck, positioning his fingers on the strings, and with his right hand he played the opening chord of "Come Together."

That night we played at Blueberry Hill, a club at which, every few weeks, Chuck Berry played. Berry had owned a restaurant called "Southern Air" outside the city, a restaurant at which, according to one former waitress, and then, later, according to almost two hundred other patrons, cameras had been installed in the women's restroom; a settlement was reached. That night in the Duck Room of Blueberry Hill, a dark and small room filled with fewer than three hundred people, a girl with beautiful legs spoke to me at the merchandise table. That night the Sixers played "Eight Days a Week" by the Beatles for Joe Murphy. Exactly eight months after that night, Joe died.

The music was life. There were times when the music quieted every drinker, every talker, every loud voice in the venue; many venues were so small that one conversation carried into the song, tried to break it. There were times when no one spoke. Times when there was nothing, because the music took them. There were other times, however, when they talked through the music, times when you could distinguish words, shouted over and through the noise coming from the amps. There were times when the music was acoustic, just strings, and still people would talk, and it was in those times when the music was not theirs; it was ours. It was ours and it took away sickness, and it took away exhaustion, and it took away fear and longing for home, and perhaps before the show we had been tired, and we had not slept, and we had driven for hours and hours and had not seen actual beds for some days, and perhaps after the show we would simply sell some albums but quickly pack and leave and, within hours of finishing, be on the interstate again, but in that space between—pavement behind us, talking heads among us, pavement in front of us—there was the music, and the music was all there was.

There was a thick red curtain behind them.

The Sixers began "Glassjaw Boxer." Boots left his drums for the mandolin, Kit left his keyboards for his accordion, and Stephen strapped an acoustic guitar around his back. Boots was stage right. Stephen was in the center. And Kit was stage left.

All three stood.

All three stood in front of microphones.

All three stood and sang: Stephen the lead, Boots and Kit the harmony.

> The chattering of businessmen
> Smug traces from the critics' pin
> They'll slap you as they smile in your face

Sam wore a dark shirt with a light tie. He was sitting at his pedal steel, bent over it at the back of the stage. The steel slid beneath the song, a long and steady whine like a metallic violin.

Through the tour he learned that he had a part to play, and though he did not always know exactly how to play it well, and though sometimes it was a minor role on stage—he was not yet singing, had no microphone, did not have a familiar stage mask with the fans as both Boots and Kit did—it was the recognition, I think, that we all noticed. In the van after the first rehearsal of the tour, Stephen had looked at Sam and said, "They want more."

We've been passed by
You know we've been passed up
Like a glassjaw boxer
Who fights for his life

On those nights when there was nothing else, music was the eleventh-hour hopeful, the mystery that brought us through the night and into each new morning. It was not always enough for the audience, but it was everything to us.

In the Pacific Northwest our van was a hospital. Kit was recovering from a throat so sore he could hardly speak, Jessica's hand was still healing from her pumpkin-carving accident, Stephen had flown home to Connecticut to recuperate from flu-like symptoms and to be with his family, and I was as congested as a sitting storm, bundled in the back of the van as we drove north through rain and night to Portland. My throat was dry; swallowing felt like ingesting razorblades. But, not allowing my sickness to deter me from the exploration of a new town, I woke early the next morning in the hotel, showered, and found an all-in-one café with coffee, breakfast, and even sandwiches and soup for lunch. I had heard much of Portland and had read that the Pacific Northwest was like another country, but I had not yet been there. It was the only major region of the United States I had not visited and it did, indeed, feel like someplace else. There were more people biking here than in Germany, more people walking than in Italy. The Asiatic cultural influx, along with, perhaps, the novelty of the West, produced something different from old Virginia or the deserts of Arizona or the lights of New York. Predictably the sky was gray, and rain would later fall, but the canopies of leaves were rusty red and smoke-tinged orange. Sitting in the café I arranged my day, which was completely open, not a single promotion gig or show. As I had been leaving the hotel Jessica, sitting in the lobby, had told me that A Fine Frenzy was playing that night at a place called the Wonder Ballroom. A Fine Frenzy was the stage name of Alison Sudol, a bright redhead with a seductively perfect and delicate voice. She played piano-pop saturated with songs of squandered love. I had never seen her live, but I had listened to her album *One Cell in the Sea* for hours after a breakup. I left the café and walked through the campus of Portland State University, stopping now and then to observe a dreadlocked cyclist or a determined businessman. The spectrum was startling.

At a center for public information an elderly woman with blonde-white hair pointed to a map, her glasses sliding down her nose, her finger tracing a route to a bus stop nearby and then across a river to a destination at which I was to get off the bus. I thanked her and walked to the bus stop.

The bus took me across the river, the city center now behind me, and dropped me off a couple blocks away from the Wonder Ballroom. The box office was closed but, walking around the corner of the building, I found an open door through which I heard some voices. People were setting up the stage for the show. I asked the general group if there were tickets still available. "Plenty," one man said. "There are *plenty* left." I wandered from Russell Street to Martin Luther King, where I crossed. I had seven hours to use before the doors were opened for the show. Standing on the street corner I saw a neon sign that said OPEN and, now hungry for lunch, my stomach burning with coffee, I entered. There were eight or nine tables and a small number of booths.

"Hello," a waiter said. There was one couple sitting at a table, and this waiter. "Sit where you like."

His voice was rather high-pitched. His blonde hair was pulled back into a ponytail. He was short and spoke the entire time in very short sentences. I sat down in a booth, placing my backpack, like company, in the bench across from me. The waiter returned with a glass of water, no ice.

"Anything else to drink?" he asked, resting his hand on the side of the booth. I said no and ordered oatmeal, deciding to pay seventy-five cents extra for sliced banana on top. I soon finished the oatmeal and ordered the "tofu scramble," a breakfast concoction of tofu, mushroom, broccoli, peppers and jack cheese. I asked the waiter how he liked Portland and what he did here and he said, oh yes he liked Portland. He danced. He looked like a dancer. He moved like a dancer through the booths and tables, holding the tray steadily. I have a friend, I said, who dances. He was vaguely impressed. And what was I doing in Portland? Was I on holiday? Business? (I would not have made a very good businessman: a thin and unkempt beard that did not quite cover half my face, torn pants, a bulging backpack.) I told him about the tour; this made him happy, and he seemed to understand something about being on the show. He lingered for a moment at the booth; yes, he knew stages and he knew the lights and he knew the audience and the spaces and people, however rare, between. We were quiet. We waited in this comfortable silence. Finally I said goodbye to the dancing waiter, who directed me to yet another café at which I could read, because I had told him of my plans to go to the Wonder Ballroom later that night and that I still needed something to do. I would have stayed there but it was closing shortly thereafter.

The next place was called Goldrush. It had dark walls and high ceilings, warm and comfortable and dry to the oncoming rain. I sat on a wooden bench facing the window, and read *A Farewell to Arms*. Two hours later Sam called.

He said he had a friend, Ryan, who was touring with A Fine Frenzy. Sam said Ryan could get us into the show free. That he could, potentially, introduce me to Alison.

"Oh," I said, on the phone in the coffee shop. "Oh yeah, oh yeah that'd be great. Wow. Really? Wow Steamer that would be awesome," I said.

I packed my bag and waited outside.

I knew Alison would fall in love with me. I had a good feeling about it. It was an obvious setup: She was a little older, weary musician type, probably grasping for someone real on the road who wasn't only after her good looks and sultry voice, and I was an ambitious young writer who had a hard time being vulnerable but who, beneath his Hemingway veneer, was gentle and soft and sweet as Skittles, a young writer who had found himself thrown into this world and was tired and was hungry for someone, hungry for something a little less lonely. I thought at least we'd start a correspondence, the momentum of which would be enough of a seed as to carry us into a romance that would affect the hearts of almost everyone in America. After all, Alison had over a million followers on Twitter! There were, realistically, only a couple things that needed to fall into place, and the first—our meeting—had miraculously materialized before my eyes. I explained my love for Alison and the destiny of our connection to the Sixers during dinner and afterward when we, Hunter Sharpless and the Sixers, smoked cigarettes.

Cigarettes had become a small and moderated ritual. It had started in Sacramento, or in San Francisco, or it had started in San Diego. Somewhere in California we had bought a pack of cigarettes and decided that smoking one cigarette each was a good way to reward ourselves for loading out so quickly. When our set was finished we had only ten minutes to evacuate the stage of everything before Tyrone's band started. The positive consequence of this hurriedness was that, after the show, we were able to leave much sooner. The negative was that those fifteen minutes were unendingly awkward—both physically, moving bulky instruments and amps off the stage while Tyrone's band moved things *onto* the stage, and also as a performance, there being neither a dramatic exit after the last song nor an encore. And it was on one of those nights that we produced a pack of cigarettes.

And we now smoked in the light rain in Portland, not as a reward but as a celebration, after which Boots and Kit dropped Sam and me off at the Wonder Ballroom.

Sam's friend had smooth, sculpted and tanned skin. He spoke with us for a while during the opener's set, and then retreated to the green room.

The Wonder Ballroom was neither wondrous nor did it resemble any sort of ballroom. There was no curling staircase. There were no Ionic columns, no murals on the wall. There was no chandelier, no statue of David, no garden, nothing. The Wonder Ballroom was simply another unimpressive venue on the road. It was a bare room, like the inside of what could have been an abandoned warehouse. There was the stage at one end and a bar at the other, and in between, splitting the center of the room like a spine, was a short partition that divided those who could drink from those who could not. Sam could have, and should have—given his predilection to fine drink—gone to the bar, and thus to the other side of the partition. But he did not. He stayed with me.

Sam had not gone to college. Speaking with him was different than speaking with either Stephen, with whom I argued Hemingway versus Dickens, or Jessica, who spoke of William Bouguereau, or Boots, who had studied film and riffed on Tarantino, or Kit, who saw in keys and measures and who wrote, in his time between tours, music for the University of Massachusetts marching band. Sam neither knew how to spell the longer words of our language—but nor did I, to be fair—nor had he read much Dickens, if any. Sam knew what he loved and he loved these things: food and drink, his wife, and music. He spoke of all these knowingly and lovingly. All created in him a similar tone of fondness and nostalgia. He had not read Dickens but he knew that Bell's Brewery in Michigan was one of the best in the country. He liked porters with overtones of vanilla, ales with pumpkin infusion. He liked wheat ales and India Pale Ales and chocolate-chip cookies. His wife's name flexed on his forearm. He never failed to ask about my family. He asked after my two younger brothers and my father and my mother. He asked after them by name. When he started talking about music he quickly lost me, but I listened. He talked about a new guitar he'd found in Nashville that had been owned by this or that musician and tweaked by this or that technician. He talked about brands and bands and history. He told me I would like Company of Thieves, and I did. He talked about his dad and his dad's band. He talked about his first band and he talked about the small studio in his basement.

A Fine Frenzy took the stage.

I had almost forgotten Alison. She was at the center of the stage now, people clapping, and she was lighted like an angel on the piano, the others in the band surrounding her; one hardly noticed them. They were only the collective frame. They were almost in total darkness. As the set progressed there were times when the room pulsed with the energetic beat of the song, and there were times when, during the heartbreaking ballads, the crowd listened, but more often than not the crowd was either talking loudly or altogether apathetic. I do not remember laughter or even a hint of a smile from Alison throughout the entire set. She did not interact with the other members of the band. And they did not interact with her. They did not participate much either in the interaction with the audience. That, apparently, was Alison's sole responsibility. And she was not enjoying it. Her face looked as though she were taking down a large pill with no candy coating. She looked lonely.

After what seemed like a very long time the show ended, and Sam and I lingered by the merch table while the audience left the building. I was plenty nervous by now. I had left my bag in the van but still wore torn pants and would have, perhaps, tamed my beard if I had known about meeting Alison. I was certainly willing to forgive her after a shit night like that on the stage, after we were hungry for her and all she did, it seemed, was pout. I understood that. If I were a musician I'd have those sorts of nights. I was the sort of person who moped often and could see myself being that way some, if not most, nights on the stage. Of course another part of me did not understand, because I had never seen the Sixers take a night off. There had been times when, moments before the music, none of us wanted to be there, times when all we wanted was to be as far away from here as possible, anywhere, but not once do I remember seeing Stephen, while taking the stage, look sorry for himself, not even in front of the sixty-five people in North Dakota, not even at promotion gigs at which there were, sometimes, as few as twelve people. Perhaps that thankfulness was a product of maturity—Stephen was years older than Alison, and he had children—but perhaps not.

Either way I was ready to forgive her if she was ready for me.

Ryan took us back to the green room, where we sat down with Omar, who also played in the band. He did not know where Alison was but said she'd be coming soon. They drank beers and I politely declined, preferring to listen to Omar's wit. He was quite funny and seemed authentically interested in my project on the Sixers. In fact, he said, Alison is writing a book. Really? I asked.

If Alison was writing a book there was surely nothing that could stop us. Omar said maybe it was a young adult fiction this or that book and I was not so much into that kind of book but if she was writing she was writing and she'd like a young writer like me, wouldn't she? I thought she would and then I heard clicking in the hallway and I knew it was her and I knew it was her high heels and then she came through the door: ripe red hair and pure white skin, slender figure and wet lips. And we met eyes, hers pulsing blue, and I quickly looked away with embarrassment as she sat down across from me but I did not fail to pay attention to the slightest movement of her body as she shook Sam's hand or crossed her legs or shifted weight and then we made eye contact again. Someone was introducing us and I was saying, "Hi," and she, "Hi," and I was holding her hand, feeling the piano-worn skin of her fingers.

Omar interjected kindly, for I had drawn short of breath and word. He told Alison that I was writing a book on the Sixers. I beamed. Yes! I was writing a book. In fact, I am a writer! She looked at me and said nothing. I heard Sam and Ryan talking.

Then I heard her say to nobody, "I wish someone would write a book about *our* band."

Sam pissed in a bottle and we took a cab to the hotel.

Less than a week before seeing the Pacific Ocean, we were in up-state New York for Halloween.

Stephen Kellogg and the Sixers dressed up as Tom Petty and the Heartbreakers. Every Halloween they covered an entire album: Pearl Jam one year, Prince another, now Petty. They had started practicing and learning the songs not too many days before the show, learning first by playing *Full Moon Fever* on repeat in the van, learning then by strumming the melodies in the van with the min-iature acoustic guitar, Kit driving, glancing in the rearview mirror at Stephen, connecting eyes, then joining in with a harmony, and learning lastly by rehearsing the songs during the sound checks in the few shows preceding that night. Quickly into this process I was singing the words of every song of this album that came out in 1989, the year I was born. They were playing the album back to front, in order to end with "Free Fallin'," and they were splitting up the lead vocals. Stephen took the lion's share, Boots and Kit each took a couple, and Sam had one song, "The Apartment Song."

There was a bat with fangs hanging from the ceiling, there were collections of cobwebs in scattered corners, there were a couple skeletons here and there, and there was a roomy electrocu-tion chair in which a zombie sat comfortably; I sat in the chair by him and watched Sam, who I had never seen sing before besides rehearsing this one song. He approached the microphone. He wore a wig of flowing hair falling past his shoulders, gray pants, a blue jacket, and sunglasses. His face tightened and he sang

> I used to live in a two-room apartment
> Neighbors knockin' on my wall
> Times were hard, I don't wanna knock it
> I don't miss it much at all

Cleveland was the last show before the last show. We had come back east. Sam and I sat across from each other eating lunch, dis-cussing my adventure the night before in Champagne, Illinois.

Four pretty coeds from the University of Illinois approached me after the show, while I was packing the stage, and asked, "So, do you ever go out after the show?" We proceeded to go to a bar called Kam's, which was full of fraternity brothers, Miller Light, and leggy girls. We stayed for twenty minutes and then went to IHOP.

Sam was proud of me.

After the show in Cleveland I drove Sam and his wife, both of whom had been drinking, to their home. I was staying the night with them before flying to Texas the next day. It was almost two in the morning when we opened their front door. I met their cat. Sam showed me his basement studio and talked about the renovations on the deck outside he wanted to make, and they offered me food. I thanked them as profusely as I could for being willing to, in less than three hours, drive me to the airport. I told Stef she did not need to wake up to ride with Sam and me as we drove there, but she did all the same.

When I retreated to coffee shops or restaurants to write I could not write. I knew I was in my own story but I had not expected correctly—if that is possible—how it would be. Books I'd read and movies I'd seen seemed to profane what was happening, except for the few good books and movies that knew how to undercut and interrupt. This was a web: constricting where I thought it would be freeing, sticky where I thought it would be clean, and finally dangerous where I thought it would be full of life. And I did not know how to write and when, later, I figured out how to write, I wondered why I wrote at all.

5

Goose

I DO NOT REMEMBER the specific airport, and I do not remember whether I was flying to the Sixers or from the Sixers. What I remember is the shrink-wrapped magazine behind the black cover on the top shelf of the newsstand, the shrink-wrap on which the words 100% REAL and MOTHER NATURE APPROVED were written. I remember buying, when walking up to the counter to purchase the *Playboy's Natural Beauties* magazine, a copy of *Sports Illustrated* to put on top, so that the middle-aged woman at the counter simply had to scan the barcode rather than see the magazine for what it was. I remember the plastic and chemical smell of the airport bathroom, the smell of old and dried piss in the stall. I closed the stall door, pulled down my pants, and took out the magazine.

Sometimes the road was day.

But sometimes, night.

Knickerbockers was two rectangular rooms at 901 O Street in Lincoln, Nebraska. They had twenty-five-cent tacos every Thursday except Thanksgiving. And they sold their award-winning spicy sauce for only four dollars. Miller Lite was on tap. So was Boulevard, and Boulevard Pale Ale. The first room of the club had a bar, a jukebox and several TVs hanging on the wall playing the afternoon college football games. The stage was in the second room, smashed at one end, along with a standing area, a few tables, and then a staircase leading to a pool table; this became our dressing room. The walls, floors, and bathrooms were wooden and dark.

The only hospitality we were given was a case of water bottles.

Knickerbockers was plain and ordinary, the sort of blank canvas the Sixers would not leave blank when they were done. After we set up I went to the bar and watched the Iowa–Penn State football game. The first quarter was almost over. As I watched, someone came over and stood by me. She was a twenty-something girl (or thirty-something woman, I wasn't sure) in a low-cut tank, exposing half her admirably large breasts.

"I thought you should know that you're going to lose," she said and smiled beneath short, jet-black hair. Her face was shiny bronze like something Egyptian. She'd probably heard me cursing as Iowa continued to make mistakes. We were down seven to zero, and Penn State was about to score again.

"What!" I said. "Not going to happen. Are you a Penn State fan?"

"Kinda." Her voice was nasally and high-pitched. "I have some friends at the game."

She looked up at the TV, and I looked down her shirt.

"Cool, cool," I said. "It looks like you're going to win right now."

They'd just kicked a field goal, and we were down ten to zero after the first quarter. I looked at the girl. We talked a little while longer. As we talked she moved close to me, angling her body around the barstool like she wanted to wrap around it. I did not ask for her name because I was a coward but also because I knew that, soon, I would be thinking between my thighs rather than between my ears. She smelled drunk and sensuous. She went to the room with the stage, a drink in hand.

My pocket vibrated. Checking my phone I saw that Silly Rabbit was almost here. Silly Rabbit was a friend I had worked with at a camp that summer in East Texas. He was a couple years older than me, had deep convictions, was full of antics and talked about writing children's books some day. I wandered over to the merch table and passed by the girl with the bronze face, and I saw that she was opening her mouth to say something to me but I turned to Jessica, who said the show was starting.

I slithered my way into a few feet of space in between a wall and the stage, by the deads. The crowd was small but excited because they had won their football game that day and had had things to drink. They wore red. I thought it was the smallest crowd we'd had so far besides Cedar Falls. A tall and thin and very pretty girl named Daisy opened the show, playing an acoustic guitar while a boy with her played a hand drum. She was awfully pretty but nervous. I wondered if it had been the nervousness that made her set so bad or just a lack of talent. While she had been playing, the crowd continued their celebration. You couldn't have blamed them. Waiting for the lights to darken and the Sixers to take the stage, I could see a TV through the doorway that was showing the Iowa game. It was exciting to watch it that way. I'd only gotten small bits and pieces of my school's games.

After Daisy's set I told Jessica that Daisy and her lovely long dark hair and her lovely skin could ride in my bunk if she wanted to come with us. Jessica said Oh yeah? I said Yes. And at the hotels Daisy could share my room if she wanted and my bed if she wanted and that would be all right if we slept together. That would be all right. Jessica frowned and said Daisy is not your type. I said Why? Jessica said she just wasn't. I said All right.

Now the lights darkened and the Sixers got on stage. Silly Rabbit found me sometime in the middle of the set, tapping my shoulder and trying to say hello through the noise. Somehow he had moved through the crowd. He was clean-shaven and his blonde hair was very short. He wore a gray shirt with athletic shorts. He'd gone to the game of course. We could not talk because the music was right by us so we only said a few sparing things very loudly into the other's ears, yelling so one might understand, and then we watched the music.

I was proud of Stephen's set list that night. It was a good, rowdy and happy bunch of Midwesterners and he'd chosen a good, rowdy and straight set for them. He kept their party going and they loved him for it. The Sixers ran and jumped around the stage, switched instruments, and when the ballads came the people quieted themselves as much as they could.

After the show Silly Rabbit and I went to the bar. It turned out he knew Daisy, the pretty, untalented girl. Silly Rabbit told me to tell her that he'd actually seen her set. To play a part in the lie. So when she came and stood by us to say hi to him, I testified falsely that he had been there. Yes, I said. Yes, I said, He saw it. Then she ordered five shots of tequila and, with the tray and the shots, standing there, she gave the impression of a cocktail waitress who'd flirt well, who'd earn a fat tip. Jessica texted and said I needed to watch the merch table for a moment, so I left them at the bar.

The girl with the bronze face walked over to the table, to me. I was nervous. She stood in front of the table, close. She was saying something to me. She was saying sweet things and she was bending over, whispering. Her breath was warm, wet. Her shirt was open inches in front of my eyes. Then feeling my hand graze her wrist, then feeling my hand drawing her close, smoothly on the curve of her hip. I could smell the alcohol and the perfume. Then saying sweet things and asking how long before I had to leave and I said about fifteen minutes and I looked at her as if to ask is that enough time? and she raised her eyebrows and asked if we were staying at a hotel nearby so that maybe I could go out with her that night and maybe I could be her boy that night and she could be my bronze Egyptian queen, but I told her the hotel was far away, outside of town.

"It is hard," I was telling Silly Rabbit when he needed to go, "to be on the road."

Hard to know what, or where, or who, was real.

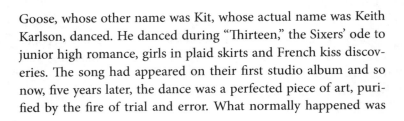

Goose, whose other name was Kit, whose actual name was Keith Karlson, danced. He danced during "Thirteen," the Sixers' ode to junior high romance, girls in plaid skirts and French kiss discoveries. The song had appeared on their first studio album and so now, five years later, the dance was a perfected piece of art, purified by the fire of trial and error. What normally happened was that Stephen, after the song had reached its crescendo and climax, would keep the rhythm going with only the acoustic guitar, behind which came, softly, the sound of Kit's voice singing, "*She's so fine / She was mine.*" Stephen would then engage the audience in a conversation, sometimes leading them to chant with him, "If you can't dance in your underpants, you don't stand a chance." And he'd look at Goose and ask, "You think you're ready?" and Goose would reply, "I certainly am," and he'd set down his bass guitar, look at the audience and throw his arms apart.

They'd cheer, and he'd dance.

But at Marilyn's on K Street in Sacramento, California, the night when Stephen was recuperating from illness thousands of miles away in Connecticut, the night when the Sixers decided against all reason to go on without Skunk, there was no one to prompt Goose into any sort of dance. Boots played the drums, Sam stood in the center of the stage with his electric guitar and Goose, smirking, stood stage left wearing blue jeans and a plaid shirt, the bass guitar strapped around his back.

The venue was a small room with a low ceiling and wooden floors. Along one length of the room was a bar; along the other was the stage, proportionally large to the size of the room, which was filled with small, wood-backed chairs and circular tables designed to give the illusion that the show was busier than it actually was. Behind the stage hung a black backdrop on which the words *Marilyn's on K* were written in sparkling gold. A shining streamer dangled over and beside the stage, framing the Sixers like a living painting. I had been asked to do merch that night, so I stood behind a table looking at an angle toward the Sixers, who were halfway through their set in front of the fewer than two hundred people who had shown up.

They were playing "Thirteen."

Throughout the set, Sam and Boots and Goose had been unable to maintain seriousness, gravity, weight, because Stephen was gone, because, though he was gone, they had decided to go on with the show, because it was Sunday night, because home was too far away to imagine, because Jessica was watching, because

I was watching, because after tonight we had two days off, because after tonight there would be Jack Daniel's, because they had decided to just play.

The crowd was complicit. They clapped, laughed, moved with the Sunday night beat. They drank cranberry-vodkas and whiskey-Cokes and they snapped photographs. They became partners in the comedic crime of a band without its frontman, without the writer of the songs, the keeper of the rhythm. I had only seen a crowd participate with this degree of purpose and single-mindedness one or two other times.

And Goose gave them what they wanted.

"Thirteen" climaxed and exhaled, reaching the lull of near silence within which it was to be decided if he'd dance or not, and he set down his bass guitar, approached the front of the stage, threw his hands open and let out a yelp.

Unbuckled his belt, unzipped his zipper, pulled off his pants.

His boxer briefs were maroon. His body was neither thin nor overweight. He was naked, and he was not ashamed. The crowd was overjoyed. Almost hysterical. The flashes of cameras. They clapped with the beat of the bass drum, with the meandering of the electric guitar. Starting the dance, Kit dropped suddenly to his knees, bent his head down, as if in prayer, spread his arms like wings and slowly raised them as the sound in Marilyn's on K intensified. Gradually he spread himself like that until, like a jack-in-the-box, at the provocation of a crash cymbal, he jumped into the air.

Wildly, he danced. To this side of the stage.

To that.

Jumped again, then landed to the crash of another cymbal. He begged the adoration of the audience, and they lauded him. They praised him, showered him. They were well pleased. And when the dance was over, he strapped the bass guitar onto his bare back and finished the song.

If Boots and I were comically pitted against each other when it came to women, Goose and I were master and disciple. The six of us had been assigned a partner for the overnight drives of the tour. Boots and Stephen were the self-named "Dream Team." Sam, who loved wordplay, said they were called this because they slept the most; this was true in the sense that the Dream Team always took the first shift of the three, generally considered the easiest, as they simply stayed awake after the show and drove for a set number of hours. Sam and Jessica took the third shift, which although was the shift likely to be the longest—if we were running late or had mismanaged time—also afforded them two shifts in a row of sleeping, the first and second. Goose and I always took the middle shift. The warrior's shift. After a show, we'd pack up, load out, and get on the road, Goose and I trying to get to sleep quickly because, three or so hours later, we'd be waking up to drive, and after three or so hours of driving, we'd again attempt to sleep. Rather than one six-hour block for sleeping, we had two three-hour blocks interrupted with Mountain Dew or gas station coffee.

In Lawrence, Kansas, it was Kit's thirty-third birthday. On the stage during the show we gave him gag gifts—the keys to the van, a water bottle, a single sock—and then started the first overnight drive of the tour, from Lawrence to Boulder, Colorado. For three hours after the show I slept, Stephen and Boots driving, and then, under the harsh fluorescent lights of a gas station, I woke to Stephen shouting, "Shift change!"

Wearing gray sweatpants and a gray cardigan, I walked into the gas station to use the restroom. I bought strawberry Pop-Tarts and whole milk and returned to the van. After appraising my selection Goose laughed.

"Well, Sharpless," he said. "Here we go."

He looked at me and grinned beneath his blonde hair.

He grew up, he said, in several New England states, finally citing Vermont as his childhood home. He remembered the smoke from his mom's cigarettes filling up the car. He went to college in Massachusetts where he met Stephen and, shortly after graduating, he became the first Sixer. His brother was in the military, stationed in Fort Hood, Texas. It seemed that they had not spoken for a very long time. The Sixers had never even met him. Kit said there was a chance his brother was coming to one of the Texas shows (he sounded at once doubtful and hopeful saying this), but when Texas came, his brother did not. He remained close to his mom, who had knit him a blanket for the tour. It was dark and porous and became my favorite in the van. Kit had been married to a girl who worked at a café in Northampton, but they were divorced a couple years back. He had once dated Stephen's hairdresser and was now engaged in a relationship with a pianist named Kathleen.

I listened to the van speeding across the asphalt and I listened to Kit describe the sudden flame he thought he had found. He and Kathleen had met not long before the tour and, given their extensive phone conversations that occurred at any point of the day or night, they already seemed quite intent on one another. When I asked the others about Kathleen, their arched eyebrows and palpable disinterest told me this had perhaps happened before.

I then began explaining my own growing list of failures with women, my cowardice and clumsiness and naiveté. I told him about Natasha, a beautiful blonde girl from Bloomington, Illinois, who used me not unlike the way she might use an emotional vibrator: away in a drawer until comfort was needed. Once, she took me out to a waterfall at a nearby lake. She had a car. I did not. It was winter. It was night. We drove out of the city and to the lake, found an empty parking lot and turned off the engine. There was the silence of the night, the roar of the waterfall, and the crunching of our feet in the snow. Our hands touched, and she told me she did not have romantic ideas about me.

Another drive with Kit, this time after Halloween, I woke with the familiar smell of gas and the clunking sound of the van doors. I bought coffee and, returning to the van, found Kit at the gas pump talking on the phone with Kathleen. She was in her mid-twenties, he was thirty-three, and it was three o'clock in the morning. She lived in Manhattan. He, when he was not on the road, lived in Amherst, Massachusetts. Like him, she played the piano. She was half Argentinean and was very close to her sister. I watched him through the window of the van. With one hand he held the phone to his ear and with the other he finished pumping gas, opened the van door, closed it, buckled his seatbelt, started the van, and pulled out onto the road. I could hear sickness taking him. His voice was low-pitched and scratchy like a dog's growl, almost the exact opposite of his normally light voice. When Kit spoke with women on the phone—Boots confided in me once, and I quickly confirmed—he deployed a unique laugh, which can only be described as a secret, murmuring, cooing affirmation leading straight into words such as "Oh, yes, you're absolutely right," or, teasing, "I'm not so sure about that," and then back into the murmurs.

He hung up the phone and said, "Man, Sharpless, I'm losing my voice."

He massaged his throat.

I thought he shouldn't participate in long phone conversations at three in the morning, but said nothing.

"I'm really into this girl," he said.

"You really like her, huh?"

"I certainly do."

It was all very strange and very fast, too strange and too fast. Later I would listen to him talk about love and love in friendship and romance and how the one person needed to sacrifice for the other, and how any relationship was a partnership rather than an act of consumption, and as I listened I was struck by the contrast between the clear lucidity and wisdom with which he spoke and the strange impulse and recklessness with which he acted.

We were listening to music in the van so that Kit would not have to use his voice when I chose "Almost Lover" by A Fine Frenzy, the song with which, after losing who I had thought was the love of my life, I simultaneously massaged and whipped my heart. I told Kit, told Kit about the girl, about the gravity I had felt in her, about the friendship, about the painting of the rocking chairs on her front porch she had made me. She was three years older. She sang, played the guitar, read books. She was pale and blonde and beautiful and she, too, called me "Sharpless," with a sisterly sort of affection. And then the disintegration, swift and total. Smoking clove cigarettes in the empty parking lot of a church at three in the morning.

When I first met Kit in Columbus, he was sitting in one of the thin-leather IKEA chairs in the dressing room with his laptop, writing an email. "Crafting" an email, he would later say, to Annie Clement, the performing bassist for the pop-country band Sugarland, for whom the Sixers sometimes opened. Annie later sat in on the Sixers' set in Nashville, wearing a plaid shirt, black tights and tall boots. She swayed back and forth with the music in front of Kit's keyboards. Like me she was the sort of person who laughed at his jokes.

Now, on the road from St. Louis to Scottsdale, Kit helped me craft a message of my own to a girl I had never seen physically but who I spent a good deal of time wooing over the Internet that fall. Her name was Rachel. We had met online when she emailed me asking about a campus organization I'd started my freshman year at the University of Iowa and which I had, because of the tour, subsequently abandoned. The group was called GoNigeria, and aimed to raise money for orphanages in the central part of the country. It was an impressive thing to have started, I thought when she emailed me, and it was all the more impressive that I was now on the road with a rock band.

Somewhere in between Missouri and Arizona, sometime in between the hours of one and eleven in the morning, the hours that spanned my and Kit's shift of the twenty-nine-hour drive that later became known to us as "The Drive," the hours during which we listened to three episodes of "This American Life" about health care and religious fanatics in Texas, Kit helped me craft a message.

"You can't be too serious," he advised as I sat in the front seat of the van, my laptop open. "But at the same time you've got to be pretty clear on what you want."

Posturing was key. You said only what you needed to.

Since we had never met, this message could be compared to a movie preview, preparing the future viewers by informing them of genre, with which there came predictable tropes and some basic plot information. Unlike a movie, though, which doesn't usually mind advertising what it actually is, I had reservations about how consistently dull and serious of a person I was, so I included in my message an obviously ironic photograph and comparison of myself to Survivorman, whose television show I had actually never seen.

This was to give the impression that I was a lighthearted and clever fellow.

Like Hemingway I wanted to suggest, in my carefully framed literature to Rachel, the possibility of affection—"Nights are hard"—the assured victory of machismo—"There's nothing like the thrill of being alone against the road"—and maybe even a deeper sort of candor—"I'm writing the road the way I see it and what the hell."

When we finally met one night many months after the tour, months of defining myself through these careful words, we sat quietly in her dorm room and discussed the strengths and weakness of the various cafeterias on campus.

When I woke early one morning in North Carolina, when I opened my eyes, I saw the curtains of the hotel room drawn nearly shut. A thin bright light, light from the rising sun, split the room in half.

The wind was cold, the sky gray and cloudy. The trees were mostly green but, the Indian summer dissolving into fall, streaks of color traced the veins of the leaves.

I did not know where I was going.

I walked on some street.

On the opposite sidewalk I saw an old man with a crown of white hair, circular spectacles, and a briefcase. I thought he looked kind. I thought he must have been a professor, since I was on the campus of the University of North Carolina. He moved slowly and amiably. I saw students with morning classes carrying their backpacks. I saw neatly trimmed yards. Somewhere on the edge of campus the buildings were very colonial-looking, with white columns and red bricks and, some of the time, green vines climbing skyward.

I changed my direction often.

I walked slowly, or I walked quickly. I breathed. I loafed. I sat down, drank coffee, and I stood up, walked more.

Then I came upon a bus stop. A man stood there alone and I asked him if the bus was free. He said it was. He was curiously vague, in age and dress and rank in society. We waited by a lamp-post. The street was wide and bending with many tall trees on either side that gave it the look of a carved, curving path that finally vanished from sight.

It started to rain.

I put my hands in my pockets.

We waited until a bus appeared around the bend.

It was nearly full. I stood near the front, my back toward the other passengers.

"Excuse me," I said quietly to the driver. I did not want the others to know I was going nowhere in particular. I asked the driver if he knew the Cat's Cradle, the venue I needed to be at in several hours. I decided I'd find out where it was and wander from there.

"Cat's Cradle, huh?" he said in a very loud voice.

He'd blown my cover.

"Yes," I said, disappointed.

He looked at me in the overhead mirror. He had light-brown hair and a mustache, very thick, of the same color. He wore a starched blue shirt with shiny buttons and a collar.

"You'll have to stay on this line for a while," he said.

His voice was very deep and loud. It did not sound like he was from North Carolina.

"You know it's closed this time of day?" he said, looking at me in the mirror again.

"I'm meeting a friend there," I lied. I did not want to explain myself.

"Oh, all right," he said.

After a while the bus was nearly empty.

"You in a band?" he asked.

"Yes," I lied again.

"What band?"

"We're called Stephen Kellogg and the Sixers."

"And the what?" he asked leaning back in his chair, angling his ear toward me.

"The Sixers."

He relaxed his position. "Never heard of them."

I said nothing.

"Where you from?" he asked.

"Massachusetts."

"Red Sox fan?"

"Not really," I said. "Our drummer is from Brooklyn. He's a Mets fan, but the rest of us aren't really baseball fans."

"What about you?" I asked. I thought I ought to ask him a question.

"Yankees fan," he said. He looked at me in the mirror with a stern expression. He was proud of being a Yankees fan.

"From New York," he said, same expression. He was an excitable fellow.

Riding the bus I heard the hum of the engine and the rattle of loose parts, the patter of the raindrops and the mechanical sound of the door opening and closing at each stop. I was fond of this bus driver the way you become fond of someone over a long while. It had seemed like a long while since I had gotten on the bus and I greatly admired his stern expression even though I was not a Yankees fan.

"What kind of music do you play?" he asked.

"Well," I said, and hesitated.

"Rock and roll?" he said, and laughed.

"Well, yeah. Like Tom Petty, or The Band."

"That's my kind of music!" He tapped his fingers on the steering wheel.

Grinned widely in the mirror.

"God bless Levon Helm and the boys," he said.

"Amen."

"You know Rick Danko?"

"Of course. We just played in Boulder and they had a picture of him. He played there."

We were quiet for a moment, and then he started singing.

"*Up on Cripple Creek she sends me, if I spring a leak, she mends me.*"

The sandy hairs of his mustache moved with the movements of his face.

I joined him, "*I don't have to speak, she defends me.*"

And we finished, "*A drunkard's dream if I ever did see one.*"

He asked more about the music and the tour. I recommended Levon Helm's biography of The Band to him and then he said that he and his friends might come to the show tonight. I shook his hand and stepped off the bus.

"Goodbye," I said. "Hope to see you at the show."

I bought a pack of cigarettes and, under an awning, the rain coming down lightly, I smoked. I smoked and I waited. Rarely was there a time on the road when I was able to distill loneliness into solitude. Rarely was I not hysterical from self-contrived conflict or sleep deprivation, or both. But there was something about the bus driver and the way he wore his mustache, which was uniquely his own, thick and sandy and moving with the contortions of his face, something about the way he sang in front of me, a stranger to him. I wondered if it was because he was a bus driver—that he interacted with so many people he no longer had the energy to put on airs, but that did not seem true, because I had spoken to bus drivers and cabbies quiet and resentful as sour clams. I wondered if he was married or if he had previously been married and I wondered if he had children and I wondered if he would come to the show and I wondered what a proud New Yorker was doing in a college town in North Carolina. I wondered whether he preferred whiskey or beer and I wondered whether his shirt was so perfectly starched because his employer, the bus company, mandated it or if the neat precision was his own doing.

In the afternoon I met with the band at the venue. Kit backed the trailer next to Carbon Leaf's van and we unloaded. Everything was dark in the Cat's Cradle: the floors, the walls, the ceiling.

Through the front door was a hallway, after which was the stage on the right and past the stage, sectioned off by a wall, the bar. It was fine to have the bar separate from the standing room. The worst venues were those where the stage and the bar faced each other, the noise reflecting and filling the space between so that neither the band nor the bartenders commanded the people. Alcohol made noise. The dressing room had two levels. Downstairs was a chair, a couch, a cooler full of Blue Moon, a table with trail mix and chips and salsa and Naked Juice, and a painting. A very triumphant-looking unicorn on its hind hooves stood on a ground of orange and yellow and red; the sky behind him was dark blue with a yellow crescent moon. Up a creaky set of stairs was a sort of loft, where there were two chairs. One was plum-colored and the other was green. The stale smell of dust was heavy. When I patted the chair the surface emitted a small but thick cloud.

It was Tuesday night. When the show started, fifteen people who had gotten home from work and had shed their work clothes and had dressed again and had driven here stood in the room. Their faces were plain and tired. The Sixers began with a song they rarely played, "All Part of the Show." On the record the song bounces beneath a backdrop of snaps. No one, however, snapped in the Cat's Cradle. On the record the song is a pop-rock toe-tapper. Tonight Stephen's microphone briefly cut out and the song did not sound like a song but more like a disenfranchised collection of discordantly disconnected pieces. I watched and tried to write what was happening. There were the facts and just because they were facts did not mean they could not be manipulated to make one thing into many things. "All Part of the Show" was two different songs. One in the studio and one in a venue. One with an engineer who had been trained and educated in how to enhance and optimize the sounds of the song, and one against the unknown of circumstance. In the studio there was the singular reverence and the meals and the collaboration and the experimentation and in the studio the song could be played and recorded over and over and layered again and again and pricked and prodded and moved forward and brought back, and then there was the stage, the stage and the way the crowd was seduced from boredom to cheers to, ultimately, and hopefully, involvement, the way they sang the words and the physical changes of expressions on their faces—taut skin, raised eyebrows, sweat—but that was only one view of the stage, because then there was the fact that when the Sixers played "All Part of the Show" on a Tuesday night in the Cat's Cradle in October of that year the song was shit, some of it being their fault—why had they chosen a song they did not even know?—and some of it being out of their control—sleep the night before, sickness, the audience, their own mood, the sound tech at the venue—and even if they anticipated and even if they had luck and even if they chose the right script for the right people these things were threats to original intention.

One was framed and the other was not.

One had the luxury of revision.

The other was spontaneous and while it could be rehearsed there were variables that could not be controlled. Control was the thing and now as they played they could not control the product when the two songs—the "All Part of the Show" of the studio, the "All Part of the Show" of the stage—were multiplied.

"All Part of the Show," however, was only the first song of the set. And perhaps because of this very reason the Sixers turned around and intensified their act—the fervor, the sweat, the engagement—until the audience roared.

When the Sixers left the stage and came into the dressing room there were high-fives and opened Blue Moons and the four bodies of the band leaning in toward one another. Someone said "Woo!" and then Stephen gave his post-show speech.

"I've never loved a crowd," he said, "as much as I loved that crowd tonight. They were bored, they were slow, and I didn't even care. We just *played*. I just wanted to give them something."

He continued, encouraging his band to always play like they did that night. From the inside out. Despite the crowd. Without notice of exhaustion. Without thought to the night. Listening to him I felt like a young boy after seeing a movie about basketball, wanting to go home and practice free throws.

Then he said, "I think we can get everywhere we want to get if we play like this."

Show after show, month after month, year after year on the road, Stephen persisted with insatiable optimism. I never knew where it was they aimed to get. And I do not know if he knew either. If it was stability, if it was record sales, if it was critical respect, if it was enough money to have a tour bus instead of a Ford van. What was enough? What was enough?—because Stephen never failed to tell me they were playing the best music of their careers. Yet the venues—the Cat's Cradle, the Blind Pig, the Cambridge Room at any location of House of Blues—were played year after year. No growth. No movement. Year after year, static.

Was static enough?

I wondered. I wondered if what Stephen told me and if what he told the crowd was true or if it was something he had convinced himself of.

The speeches sobered. Kit mentioned the recent trip to the Middle East the Sixers had taken, playing for deployed American troops. Changed the way they played, he said. There were nods. St. Jude fundraising, elementary schools, hospitals. Was altruism enough? Why did they play? And what was it they wanted so badly?

Then I heard: "I'm drinking tonight!" It was Kit, who had not been drinking that tour.

This encouraged Sam.

There was chanting.

They chanted in the van and I kept quiet. We drove to the hotel and I volunteered to take Kit's suitcase into our room because he was going to a bar with Sam and some others. Jessica asked if I would get up in the morning and fill the parking meter. I was reluctant at first, difficult, but finally I said yes. It was very dark outside. It was cold. I got Kit's bulky suitcase from the trailer. He waited for me. I pulled out my cigarettes and offered him one. He took it. We lit them. We stood in the cold with our cigarettes.

"Hunter," he said, "it's been really cool to have you out on this tour. It's made it really special."

I exhaled smoke and looked away so he wouldn't see my embarrassed smile.

I said thank you. I wanted to say something that would be honest but not overly sentimental. I knew what I wanted to say, but I didn't know how. I felt very close to everyone in the band and to Jessica but with Kit there was something very unique about our shifts together, talking of girls who had broken our hearts, crafting messages to try to woo girls hundreds of miles away, listening to music together, him meeting my family, him telling me of his own brother and mother.

"I know I've said this before," I began.

I took another drag.

"Oh shit!" he said.

He looked past me to the sidewalk where Sam stood.

I had wanted to say he felt like an older brother.

"I've got to go," he said. "But I'll see you in the room!"

Throwing his unfinished cigarette down, he jogged over to Sam.

Standing in the cold, I finished mine.

I had wanted to tell him that I was a good older brother. It was what I had known since I was young and I was the forger even if I dutifully followed the rules and I was conscious of not stepping off the path. I'd never had the freedom to stop looking at my own feet—which in a way determined the path of my brothers behind me—and look ahead to those who'd lived.

I went back to the room and took my clothes off. I looked in the mirror and then put them on again. I wanted to walk.

There was a knock at the door.

"Here," Jessica said. She handed me a bag full of quarters for the meter in the morning. She looked at me skeptically.

"What are you doing?"

I told her I was going for a walk.

"Are you okay?"

I said that I was.

"Are you sure?"

I said that I was.

She hesitated a moment, holding the door open, looking at me, but then she left.

The beds were made-up and there were two pieces of chocolate on each, and using an unread newspaper I made an arrow pointing to the chocolate pieces and then wrote a note on a piece of paper, leaving it for Kit and Sam when they would come back.

Outside it was cold, dark and quiet. I roamed the streets, dark streets, lighted streets, busy streets, streets with bars, streets with fraternity houses, empty streets. When I was walking it was not cold because my body was moving, but when I sat down on a bench after buying a sandwich it was very cold in the wind and without the movement, so I ate quickly and lit a cigarette. I smoked three before getting up and lighting another. Then I heard a voice across the street.

"Excuse me, sir," the voice said. It was an old woman.

I crossed the street to her. She was very small, not five feet. She had a wrinkled face and brown eyes that wandered, unfocused, shooting about in different directions, avoiding my eyes directly but looking all around me. Her big, stained, white shirt flapped in the wind like a flag. She must have been very cold.

"Buy me a drink?" she asked.

It was past midnight.

"Can I buy you a sandwich?" I said.

"I'm cold," she said.

Her feet shifted underneath her.

"Can I buy you a sandwich?" I repeated. "Look, there's a place right there."

I gestured to it.

"I need a drink."

Her eyes spun.

"You don't need a drink."

Her eyes were here and then gone.

"You don't need a drink," I said again.

"I'm cold, sir. I need a drink. Buy me a drink?"

She kept saying she needed a drink and I tried to lead her to the sandwich shop, angling my body between her and the shop, open to her, trying to encourage her, but she stood motionless. I walked away and looked over my shoulder, her flag of a shirt flapping in the wind, and looking again she was still there, and wearing flip-flops, and her shirt torn, and standing on the curb, and then standing in the street, and all the while looking around me as if the world existed but something escaped the center, and then on the sidewalk, and then the street, and all the while saying can I have a drink buy me a drink would you buy me a drink. I felt the nicotine in my blood and it warmed me but I was still cold.

In the room Kit and Sam were very drunk. The note that I had left them was on the floor. There was a note written by someone that said something. I threw it on the floor and got in bed. They were talking about some woman's chest.

Someone said she had great breasts.

The other agreed.

And I went to sleep.

In the dressing room before every show the Sixers would decide that night's "unifying factor," some color scheme or accessory in common that would visually unite them. For example, every now and then when this moment arrived one of them might look up from their wardrobe bag and say, "Brown town?" in which case they'd all wear something brown. Sometimes, they all wore plaid. Sometimes, a tie. Sometimes, a fedora. Each night was different.

One night at the Visulite Theater, as we sat in the dressing room pondering what might be that night's unifying factor, Kit burst out of the restroom, threw his arms open and said, "What about *this*!"

He wore blue jeans and, over his bare torso, a vest.

We all looked at him.

And then, inexplicably, that far-off look of half-serious consideration entered Stephen's eye, and what at first had presumably been a joke became something plausible, which gave way to the incarnation—with a twist—of Kit's original idea: They were to all wear vests *under* plaid, buttoned shirts, which they were to dramatically discard following Stephen's lead during the song "Thirteen."

The Sixers were giddy as schoolboys.

We can do this! they thought.

They will love the vests! they said of the audience.

This is so *us*.

When the time came and Kit, the front-runner, ripped off his shirt, revealing very white shoulders and a very dark vest, the audience, after some confusion, clapped very modestly. After Sam revealed himself, they seemed suspicious. After Boots, they still applauded but the process was taking longer than they would have liked, and it looked as though the applause had been demanded of them. And when Stephen—whose entire body sprawled with dark wiry hairs—took off his shirt, they looked rather horrified.

The Sixers themselves, along with Jessica and me, were the only people laughing.

"This is our last shift," I said.

I looked at Kit, behind the wheel of his sedan. Boots and Sam were asleep in the back seat.

"I guess you're right, Sharpless," he said, keeping his eyes on the road.

Brooklyn was in front of us, the point of departure. Sam would fly home. Kit would drive home. I would fly home. And Boots would already be home. Last night we had stayed at Stephen's in-laws' house in Greenwich, Connecticut. Last night had been New York, when I had vomited and with one decisive and dramatic action had abolished my reputation as a dry fellow. I had opened the front door and Kirsten, Stephen's wife, had washed my stomach fluids off my jacket and the next morning I woke feeling absolutely all right, because I had expelled everything so quickly, the Red Stripe and the Maker's Mark. Now it was Brooklyn. Now it was home. In the car on the road we listened to *Heartbreak Warfare* by John Mayer and ate leftover cupcakes from a clear plastic container. We talked about how much I had drunk the night before and the things that stood out as mile markers on the road. The diner waitress who, while serving eggs and bacon and coffee and pancakes and syrup, read Kit's mind. We remembered one shift, while I was playing DJ, that I switched from Rage Against the Machine to Joss Stone. "What!" Kit had said when I turned her song on. "This is your jam, Sharpless?" I sang the words and danced in the passenger seat of the van. It was my jam. We remembered that in Iowa, before I gave my speech about how the Sixers were like older siblings to me, I talked to Kit first, because I was afraid. And he encouraged me, told me to go ahead with it. We remembered that at Shank Hall in Milwaukee, when I was confined to fifty square feet of space, I was slamming and throwing and hitting cases after the show while we packed. "Hey," Kit had said, resting his hand on my shoulder. I had not seen him. "You okay, pal?" We remembered driving through Vermont in the heat of autumn, the billowing hills a sea composed of fiery orange trees. In the van no one spoke until Kit said to me, "I could see you living here." I had asked if he really thought so and he said yes and I was full of hope. We remembered Nebraska. We had been driving on Interstate 80 and were not many miles from the exact center of the United States. My hair was matted and oily and in my armpits were cream-colored clumps of deodorant. I'd slept four hours and now was looking out the van, which seemed small. In each direction was a vast, expansive view. The land was flat and colored like a new canvas by corn and wheat, and the sky was growing clearer with the light. It was Saturday afternoon. When we parked the trailer I took a walk because I had been asked to find us coffee. In Nebraska, people from all corners of the state drove into town for the football game. There were college girls in jean shorts with red stickers on their cheeks. There were whole families with parents maneuvering strollers through hoards of drunk and soon-to-be-drunk college students. There were children. There were people eating, people drinking, and people tailgating. There were people at bars. People talking about the game before the game. Speculating, betting, wagering. Thinking, hoping, knowing. There were people talking about other football games across the country. There were people throwing footballs. People tossing beanbags. People cooking. People in overalls. The city swelled, and while I walked through it wearing lime green pants, a deep-cut shirt, and a wiry beard, the people berated me. They heckled me. Jeered at me. Cursed. They called things out from the top floors of parking garages and corners of intersections. They laughed at me. Pointed at me. Called me a clown. Raised eyebrows after seeing me. Whistled at me. They had quite a time with me. But I knew towns like this. They were part of me.

The expression is determined both by the person on the other end and by the intention of the expression itself. If what I am writing is meant to convey the unframed road— the coffee and the night and the asphalt—then does the necessity of revision taint the original intention? I frame in order to suggest the unframed. I recant, recall, reapportion, reassess, rebuild, rewrite, rework. What was once disorder I have reconstructed in order, in order to evoke what I felt in the beginning: hunger.

Acknowledgments

I am grateful to many people:

My parents, for financing my KIA rental car, and for loving me. My brothers, for putting up with me. A great many teachers who have, in some way large or small, and whether they have realized it or not, helped me: John D'Agata, Kristen Radtke, Cutter Wood, and David Hamilton. Ed Folsom and his class on Walt Whitman. Cafés and bars across the country, but mostly Donnelly's in Iowa City.

I'd like to especially thank my final readers: Andrew Hoogheem, a fine writer and teacher and a better man; Elena Carter, a great roommate in Minneapolis whose work will be forthcoming sometime soon; and Brian Deutschendorf, who has been a faithful and loyal friend and reader since I walked into his advising office at the University of Iowa six years ago.

Brooks Landon was the first one who believed that I could really do this. His door was always open. He encouraged patience and hard work, and I'm thankful.

Of course, the Sixers themselves: Kit, Sam, and Boots, for being like brothers to me, for tolerating the insecure young man I was, for helping me grow up. Jessica, the sister I never had. Stephen, for letting the whole thing happen, and for writing the foreword.

Anders Holine, for doing outstanding design work without a penny's wage.

Stefanie Pinkney, who not only copyedited this book for the meager price of a bottle of bourbon but who provided many other suggestions, and who I am lucky to call a friend.

Joshua Casteel, who passed away in 2012, and who I knew only briefly, but who gave and gives me the courage to call myself a writer.

Marissa, my love, who has helped guide this project on both the editorial and marketing fronts, and who happens to be the best woman I know.